DISCERNING GOD'S PLAN FOR YOU

Jeffrey O. Cerar

To Chris, a servant who has touched many lives.

Jeff

Northumberland Historical Press

NHP

Northumberland Historical Press
Heathsville, VA

Scripture taken from the Holy Bible,
New International Version
© 1973, 1978, 1984 by International Bible Society.
Used by permission of Zondervan.

Cover Photo of the cloister at Salisbury Cathedral in
Salisbury, England. Used by permission.

ISBN-10: 0-9979846-2-7
ISBN-13: 978-0-9979846-2-0

Library of Congress Control Number: 2017950351

Printed in the United States of America

CONTENTS

INTRODUCTION

The premise of this book is that God has a plan for every believer. When I say that, I do not mean that God has scripted your life in every detail. If that were so, God's will and God's power would assure that you are never off script. In that case, there would be no point in seeking to discover God's plan for you.

Rather, I'm saying that God made you with a particular purpose for your life. He has given you certain gifts. He has prepared you in certain ways. He has made you a responsible agent of his grace to be free to choose his way. We know that "God desires that no one should perish" (2 Peter 3:9), yet some choose to reject his gift, his grace, his salvation; in the same way, he has a plan for each of us, but some will choose to reject that plan. This book is for the seekers among us who want to discern God's plan for them because they love the Lord and want to live as God desires.

Some people love the Lord but have never considered that he has a specific plan for them. They may try their best to live by the commands of Jesus, responding in a godly way to the things that happen in their lives. This is to be celebrated. But to live the Christian life this way short changes the believer from the full richness, joy and satisfaction that could be theirs. They may find themselves doing good deeds but not feeling fulfilled. They may do many acts of charity but think, as Os Guiness testified in his book, *The Call*, "But it just wasn't me."[1]

What this says is that even those who don't believe God has a plan for their lives must engage in discernment. At the very least, they have to decide, "How can I be Christ's witness and show his love in a way that matches my gifts and experience?" The New Testament is clear that God gives the disciple spiritual gifts to be used for God's work (1 Corinthians 12, Ephesians 4:11-13). Does it not make sense that the One who gave us those gifts should be the One to say how they should be used and what good should come out of them?

Moreover, how do you sort out the various claims on your time and energy? There are so many needs. Anyone who becomes known as a good person is besieged by requests. How are we to know what to say "yes" to, and what to say "no" to? We have to decide. We have only so much time. We have a family to nurture; we have a job; we need our rest; we need recreation and refreshment; we need time for prayer and Bible study. We can't do everything that comes our way, and if we try, we become disillusioned. And what are you to think when well-intentioned people,

---

[1] Os Guiness, *The Call* (Nashville: Thomas Nelson, 2003).

seeing the spark of faith in you, encourage you to redirect your life altogether—become a missionary or a pastor? Does their urging amount to a call from God? Or is it simply that they have too narrow a view on what a call from God is? How do you know which is the case?

As God's people have discovered over and over through the centuries, from the days of Noah until today, once we submit to God, we find that we are not limited by what we know we are able to do. God often calls us to tasks and vocations that we would never have dreamed of—callings that we think are beyond our capabilities and outside our gifts. And there we find great treasure. For when we are outside our safe zone, knowing God has brought us there and relying on the Holy Spirit to give us what we need, we experience joy and fulfillment that we never thought possible. "No eye has seen, no ear has heard, no mind has conceived what God has prepared for those who love Him" (1 Corinthians 2:9).

It is my hope that this book will help Christians find direction in the fulfillment of their desire to serve God. The goal is to glorify God and thereby find the joy and satisfaction that he intends for those he loves.

Chapter 1

GOD HAS A PLAN

*C*hristians' lives are not our own. We are followers of the Master who said, "If anyone would come after me, he must deny himself and take up his cross and follow me" (Matthew 16:24). Jesus was showing his disciples the hard road he would travel and signaling that their lives too would be difficult. He was also signaling that he has expectations of those who would be his followers. The questions this raises are: What is your cross? How specific are God's expectations? How personalized are those expectations to the life of each of his followers? Does God have a plan for your life?

The serious disciple of Jesus Christ will ask from time to time, "Am I doing what the Master wants me to do?"

- Maybe you are a college student, surviving the faith-challenging environment of modern academia and looking ahead to the future. You have seen firsthand how critically important it is that Christians live as Jesus commands. But you wonder: "Where should I go? What should I do? How shall I invest the gifts my Creator has given me? Surely God has a plan for me."

- Or maybe you are a missionary who has just returned from twenty years in Turkey. The doors have been closed to you there. You know that your time there has come to an end. You are back home in the United States, still in your recovery period. What comes next? You want to serve the Lord faithfully with everything you have. But how? Should you go back into the mission field? Should you train others to be missionaries? Should you get involved in management of a mission agency? Or should you go in another direction completely? What is God's plan for you?

- Or suppose you have just gotten out of prison. Your youth was a seething cauldron of bad companions, ill-conceived schemes and deplorable goals. The law caught up with you and sent you to prison for twelve difficult years. But it was there, on a Kairos weekend,[2] with a team of trustworthy Christians bringing the saving word of Jesus Christ to you and forty-one other men, where you came to know the truth about life, about God, about the world, and about yourself. You gave your life to Christ. And now, you are looking at the blank slate

---

[2] Kairos Prison Ministry International is a Christian organization whose mission is "to share the transforming love and forgiveness of Jesus Christ, to impact the hearts and lives of incarcerated men, women and youth, as well as their families, to become loving and productive citizens of their communities." (www.kairosprisonministry.org)

of a new life. What should you do? You know God saved you on purpose. It was his doing. He picked you to become his child. Surely he has a plan for you.

- Or suppose you are not at a major turning point. You're just a Christian who has been worshiping week by week, volunteering in a women's shelter, attending Bible study, and living a Christ-like life as best you can. As you lie in bed at night thinking about your love for Jesus, you wonder, "Am I doing what he wants? Does he have a plan for me that I have not yet discovered? Has this ministry been preparing me for something else?"

We know that Jesus gave his disciples definitive marching orders. He said, "You shall be my witnesses...to the ends of the earth" (Acts 1:8). And he said, "My command is this: Love each other as I have loved you" (John 15:12). God's plan for us, then, is to be Christ's witnesses and to love one another with the same self-giving love Jesus has for us. Taking up your cross could mean simply living, as best you can, the kind of life those commands entail. J.I. Packer has warned us to be cautious of impressions and knowledge that we perceive as being God's revelation to us personally. "There is no certain way to test such impressions," he says. "Sometimes one will not be able to tell whether they are a message from God or a human fancy. The correct conclusion to draw is that we seek to do what by biblical standards best serves

God's glory and the good of others, God will be with us—just that."[3]

But does "take up your cross and follow me" mean nothing more than following the biblical standards for discipleship? If that is true, then the fulfillment of God's plan of redemption is at the mercy of his disciples, contingent upon how wise we are about choices and strategies, and on how willing we are to act.   Yet we are all sinners.   "All have sinned and fall short of the glory of God" (Romans 3:23). It seems self-evident that God has a better use for us than to leave his sinful followers to decide when and how to glorify him and advance his kingdom.

> **The Bible attests to the plans God expressed in the lives of his leaders and prophets of old.**

We see evidence in the Bible that God has a plan specific to each one of us. The first view the Bible gives us of God's plan to redeem the world is his personal call on the life of Abraham.   He informed Abraham in Genesis 12 that he had a plan not only for Abraham but for the entire world. It was God's plan that Abraham go to a land God would show him and settle there.   Abraham and his barren wife Sarah would have a baby in their old age. (Abraham was already seventy-five when

---

[3] J.I. Packer, *God's Plans for You* (Wheaton, IL: Crossway, 2001), 106.

he set out for the land God would show him.) From that child would come descendants as numerous as the sands of the seashore. And through Abraham's descendants, the entire world would be blessed (Genesis 12:1-3, 15:4-5).

You may say that God's selection of certain people to be instrumental in his plan of redemption does not necessarily mean that he has a plan for you. But Abraham's call was not an isolated incident. It illustrates a pattern of how God has worked throughout history.

In the biblical account, God came to people with a call upon their lives. He did not simply wait for them to do something and then make good things come from it. He pursued them. He spoke to them. He demanded something very specific from them. In fact, many of them resisted, equivocated, even argued with God in some cases. God clearly had a plan for them:

- Noah, who built the ark for the righteous to survive a worldwide flood:

  > So God said to Noah, "...I am going to destroy all life under the heavens, every creature that has the breath of life in it. Everything on earth will perish. But I will establish my covenant with you, and you will enter the ark." (Genesis 6:13-18)

- Moses, the fugitive murderer, whom God appointed to lead his people from slavery in Egypt to the Promised Land:

> [The Lord said to Moses] "And now the
> cry of the Israelites has reached me, and
> I have seen the way the Egyptians are
> oppressing them. So now, go. I am
> sending you to Pharaoh to bring my
> people the Israelites out of Egypt."
> (Exodus 3:9-10)

- David, the shepherd boy whom God made king:

  > The Lord said to Samuel, "…I am sending
  > you to Jesse of Bethlehem. I have
  > chosen one of his sons to be king."
  > …[Jesse] sent and had [David] brought
  > in. He was ruddy, with a fine appearance
  > and handsome features. Then the Lord
  > said, "Rise and anoint him; he is the
  > one." So Samuel took the horn of oil and
  > anointed him in the presence of his
  > brothers, and from that day on the Spirit
  > of the Lord came upon David in power. (1
  > Samuel 16:1-13)

- The prophets, who interrupted their lives to speak the very words of God:

  > The word of the Lord came to me, saying,
  > "Before I formed you in the womb I knew
  > you, before you were born I set you apart;
  > I appointed you as a prophet to the
  > nations."
  > "Ah, Sovereign Lord," I said, "I do not
  > know how to speak; I am only a child."
  > But the Lord said to me, "Do not say,' I
  > am only a child.' You must go to everyone

> I send you to and say whatever I command you." (Jeremiah 1:4-7)

- Mary, the young virgin whom God called to be the mother of the Savior:

> ...God sent the angel Gabriel to Nazareth, a town in Galilee, to a virgin pledged to be married to a man named Joseph, a descendant of David. The virgin's name was Mary. ...the angel said to her, "Do not be afraid, Mary, you have found favor with God. You will be with child and give birth to a son, and you are to give him the name Jesus. He will be great and will be called the Son of the Most High. The Lord God will give him the throne of his father David, and he will reign over the house of Jacob forever; his kingdom will never end." (Luke 1:26-33)

- The disciples, whom Jesus trained and sent out into the world to share the Good News:

> [Jesus said to his disciples] "You did not choose me, but I chose you and appointed you to go and bear fruit—fruit that will last. (John 15:16)

> "You will receive power when the Holy Spirit comes on you, and you will be my witnesses in Jerusalem, and in all Judea and Samaria, and to the ends of the earth." (Acts 1:8)

- Saul of Tarsus, the persecutor of Christians whom God turned into an unequalled evangelist, apologist and theologian:

> [Jesus said to Saul] "I am Jesus, whom you are persecuting... Now get up and go into the city, and you will be told what you must do." The Lord said to Ananias, "This man is my chosen instrument to carry my name before the Gentiles and their kings and before the people of Israel. I will show him how much he must suffer for my name." (Acts 9:5-16)

Psalm 139 tells us God knew us before we were even knit together in our mother's womb. "When I was woven together in the depths of the earth, your eyes saw my unformed body. All the days ordained for me were written in your book before one of them came to be" (Psalm 139:13-16). If the creative God, who makes all things and knows all things, knew us before we even came to be, and if he has expectations of us, then it is reasonable to assume that he has plans for us.

> **It is God's initiative, God's work, and God's plan that we are witnessing here.**

The message is not at all hidden from our view. God uses the people he created in order to accomplish his will. When you consider the qualifications of those in the Bible for whom God had a plan, you see right away that they were no more worthy than we ordinary people who follow God today. All were sinners—some egregiously so. Many were reluctant. Most thought they didn't have the necessary gifts. But God knew what he was going to do. And he knew he was going to make possible what would have been impossible without the power of his Holy Spirit working in them, doing infinitely more than they could ask or imagine (Ephesians 3:20). Clearly, it is God's initiative, God's work, and God's plan that we are witnessing here. And his Word contains nothing to remotely suggest that he doesn't have the same kind of plans for each of us. Philippians tells us:

> Continue to work out your salvation with fear and trembling, for it is God who works in you to will and to act according to his good purpose. (Philippians 2:12-13)

This is a call to recognize that we are vessels for God's gracious redeeming work—but not just passive vessels. "Working out our salvation" means to stay active and engaged with God's work in us, moving along his path from being saved to living great lives. "Fear and trembling" refers to the urgency and critical nature of the things God is doing through each of us. This requires that we be alert to what God may be saying to us.

Jesus said that he brings eternal life to all who believe in him, a life that goes on forever in the presence of God. Immortality is something human beings have long sought after. But a life that goes on forever can be wonderful or horrible, depending upon the quality of that life. The quality of the life Jesus promises to the believer sets it apart from all else. Life with Jesus is an intimate relationship with the One who is love itself, who embodies the truth, who manifests goodness in all he does. It is an every-moment closeness with the One who spoke a word and the whole cosmos came to be. For the believer, eternal life begins in the here and now, and the potential of that life is so glorious that it cannot even be compared to the unredeemed life. When we are living into God's plan for us, that quality of life bursts forth like Jesus from the tomb.

* * * * *

In 2004, my wife Lynne and I accepted a call to join a mission team to Kenya. The mission, sponsored by Sharing of Ministries Abroad, was to work with the Anglican Archbishop of Kenya by leading a nationwide clergy retreat that would kick off a year of revival. Almost one hundred missionaries were involved. Once we arrived in Kenya, we spent a week preparing and then headed out in teams of eight to the twelve regions of Kenya.

The team I was asked to lead was sent to Mombasa, a city on the east coast. It was a daunting mission for several reasons. First, we did not have the full complement of team members.

There were only five of us. Second, among the five, only Lynne and I, and a young Ugandan layman, were willing to teach; we were to lead a series of five day-long sessions. Third, there was no pre-set curriculum; it was up to our team to create the entire program. Fourth, there was no money in the budget of the Anglican Church in Mombasa because a famine had caused the Bishop to spend all his available funds on feeding the hungry. And finally, the Church along the east coast of Kenya was very much on edge. The Christians were afraid of the Muslims because of recent terrorist activity against the churches. I had never felt so inadequate or had so many blank pages in my playbook. Never had I prayed with such urgency for God to do miracles and to show us the way.

> *For the believer, life with God begins here and now, and takes its quality from the life of God, which he shares with us.*

God had a plan, and he had it all in hand. One of the miracles we encountered was that Lynne and I had raised far more money for our trip than our personal expenses required, and we had brought the extra funds with us. It turned out to be just enough to pay for the whole conference. But the biggest miracle was that our young teammate from Uganda was exactly the person needed to fill the empty spots in our five-day conference. The people of Mombasa and the east coast knew almost nothing about Islamic doctrine.

All they knew was that the terrorists were to be feared. Our Ugandan was a man who had an encyclopedic knowledge of the Qu'ran, the Arabic language, and the Bible, and he had a burning zeal to share what he knew with Christians. The conferees went away on the last day much encouraged, strengthened and confident. And one pastor from the remote northeastern coast, who had arrived defeated, bitter and afraid, left the conference filled with the Holy Spirit, singing God's praises, and eager to get back to his congregation to pass on the blessing.

* * * * *

Our experience in Mombasa demonstrated three things to me about God's plans. First, when we are in tune with God's plan for us, we come to know God better. We know him better, because we have a more intimate grasp of what the Bible means when it says God is redeeming the world. As we play a part in that redeeming work, we see the patterns of God's goodness and creativity, his love and patience. We also come to know God better while we are engaged in his plan for us, because we must turn to him constantly in prayer, seeking his strength and guidance. Since it is his plan and not ours, we rely on what he says. And with that frequent, urgent and intimate conversation comes a deepening of our relationship with God.

Second, when we are in tune with God's plan for us, we live a full and rich life. The things that beckon our attention will be more and more the things of God. Our perspective changes. The things that satisfy and delight us, the things that give us joy, the things we would do anything to keep, will be more and more the things for which God made us—to praise him and enjoy His presence forever.

Third, when we are in tune with God's plan for us, we see miracles. As we move through life in a daily existence influenced by the world, the flesh and the devil, we take for granted the great things God does. We allow them to be explained away. We discount them. But when we are walking closely with God in the work he is doing through us, we see the truth. We see the things that never would have happened were it not for the hand of God. We see our own inadequacy being overcome by God's power. As written in Philippians 4:13, "I can do all things through him who strengthens me." We see "coincidences" turn into creative moments: "God works all things together for good for those who love him and have been called according to his purpose" (Romans 8:28).

God has plans for each one of his disciples, and it is therefore of utmost importance that we listen for his voice, hear him, and follow his lead. Be aware, however, that discerning God's plan for you is not a one-time thing. It's not as if God says, "You are to be an apologist in academia. Get to it.

Have a nice life." Knowing God, heeding His call, and seeking his direction should be a life-long practice. The years we spend on this earth as disciples of Christ are replete with major directional decisions and small tactical choices. Walking in God's pathway the whole way ought to be our aspiration. And indeed, it will become our heart's desire as we discover how precious is the intimacy we gain with him by constantly seeking to hear from him.

Embarking on a quest to discern God's plan is not something to be undertaken casually. Once you know that God wants you to pursue some course of action, you will not be able to rest as long as you remain out of his will. And it will require a great deal of you: obedience, courage and holiness of life. But you will not walk alone. You will have the Holy Spirit to guide you, empower you, and encourage you. And you will have the joy of participating in God's great work of redeeming the world. You will experience the treasure of a rich and purposeful life with Him.

Chapter 2

ACHIEVING QUIET

*H*ave you ever been reading the Bible and found after several paragraphs that you didn't know what you had read? Sometimes, we have to read the same paragraphs multiple times before we truly pay attention. Where is one's head at those times? It could be just about anywhere.   We have so many distractions that it is difficult to focus: the petty worries of the day; the troubling news of world events; the things on our to-do list; the upcoming vacation; the decisions we must make; the people we need to call; the pets we need to take in for their shots; the pot of soup bubbling on the stove. And then, of course, there is all the electronic paraphernalia that beckons for our attention: cell phone, laptop, i-pad, e-reader, social media, text messages. If it seems all this distracts us when we are reading, the same is true in our praying. The things spinning in our heads make it almost impossible to hear from God when he is speaking to us.

How do we free ourselves up to listen to God? Seeking to hear from God is more a process than an event. The process needs to be seen as a season, rather than a single prayer session. God does not always answer right away. And he doesn't always speak

> *In order for this time to be focused and productive, we need quiet and freedom from distractions.*

to us in obvious ways, although most Christians report that what initially seemed obscure was later seen in retrospect as more like God hitting them between the eyes with a two-by-four.

It is best to think of discerning God's will as a campaign. A campaign requires adequate preparation. That preparation is a collection of spiritual disciplines, all of which are aimed at humbling ourselves before God, and quieting our hearts and minds so as to focus deeply on Him. The seeker needs to plan a season of prayer, worship, Bible reading, meditation and possibly fasting. Each of these disciplines needs to be a matter of regular practice. During such a campaign, you should not miss any opportunity to be in corporate worship with your fellow Christians. If your church has a worship service on Christmas Eve and another on Christmas day, don't temporize over which would be better to attend. Go to both, and give thanks that God has offered you two times to worship him. Regular prayer, Bible study, and meditation should be a matter of committed time at least every day. The three go hand in hand. Prayer leads us into Scripture, and reflecting on Scripture is an essential bridge to understanding what the Word of God is saying, both generally and to each of us as individual disciples.

For this time to be focused and productive, we need quiet and freedom from distractions. The first thing is to shut off all the devices that could beep or ring or tweet, so that we won't be tempted to answer them and so that we won't even wonder who might be seeking our attention. These electronic communicators are more intrusive than we give them credit for. Not only do their bells and beeps interrupt, but even the anticipation of them pulls at us. The consideration of what we are going to say in response fills our heads. Escaping their nagging influence is essential for quiet time with God.

It also helps to be in a place where little else is going on. Missionaries report that God often awakens them at three o'clock in the morning to speak to them. (It must be a favorite time of his!) For some people, non-busy quiet means not even music. For others, music can be a quieting, focusing influence. The same is true of visual distractions. Some need to close their eyes or pray in the dark. For others, walking in the woods or sitting by a meadow or stream helps them listen to God. The key is that your heart and mind are focused peacefully on the One whose words you cherish.

How many times in the Gospels do we see Jesus going off to a place of solitude to pray?

Sometimes he prayed early in the morning (Mark 1:35). Sometimes he prayed all night (Luke 6:12). Often we find him praying alone on a mountainside (Luke 9:28). When he taught his disciples to pray, he urged them to go into their room, close the door, and be with the Father in private (Matthew 6:6). Just before he ascended into heaven, he told his disciples to go into Jerusalem and wait until they had been clothed with power from on high (Luke 24:49).

A. W. Tozer urges the Christian to find solitude, for, "There is a place where the mind quits trying to figure out its own way and throws itself wide open to God."[4] That, it seems, is what God was pushing Elijah to do when he ran away from Queen Jezebel. It was there, in a cave high on a mountainside, that God came; speaking in a still, small voice, he laid out for Elijah the plans he still had for him (1 Kings 19).

Elijah thought he had it all figured out. He had done his utmost for God. Ahab and Jezebel had introduced the worship of the pagan god Baal. The Israelites had given over their loyalty to this false god. Elijah had set up an astounding test of God's power against the power of Baal. God had triumphed in dramatic fashion. And yet, hearts were not turned, and the queen swore to kill Elijah.

---

[4] A.W. Tozer, *Culture: Living as Citizens of Heaven on Earth* (Chicago: Moody Publishers, 2016), 101.

Elijah was sure there was nothing else to be done. He was certain he was the only faithful prophet left. He fled and wanted to die a peaceful death at God's hand, not at the sword of Jezebel. As he lay under a tree to die, he was awakened by an angel, who sent him on to Mt. Horeb. And hiding in fear inside that cave on the mountainside, he was alone with God. God revealed that Elijah was not the only faithful one left; he gave the prophet specific orders for where he was to go next and what he was to do. Elijah had quit trying to figure out his own way. He was now wide open to God—alone, quiet, listening. And then God spoke.

Chapter 3

GIVE GOD THANKS AND PRAISE

"**O** for a thousand tongues to sing my dear Redeemer's praise." This great hymn by Charles Wesley comes from the heart of a believer who knows and loves the Lord so much that he cannot contain his praise. There is never a time when it is inappropriate to praise God. One especially fitting time is when you begin a season of seeking God's face and asking him to show you his plan for you. A thorough inventory of all the things about God that cause us to worship him and of all the things he has done for us personally as his children, prepares us in several ways to hear from him. First, it reminds us that we are speaking with none other than Almighty God, as his creatures totally dependent on him. Second, it energizes our love for him, which makes us all the more ready to learn his plan and his will for us—and to please him by putting ourselves at his disposal. And third, we find that as we rehearse the ways God has blessed us, we gain insight about how he has been preparing us for his service. Often, our eyes are opened to God's plan even at this early stage.

If we begin at the beginning, we praise God simply for who he is:

- God is good.
- God is love.
- God is faithful.
- God is eternal.
- God—Father, Son and Holy Spirit—is the only God.
- God is perfect in his knowledge.
- He is infinitely wise.
- God is all-powerful.
- God is endlessly creative.
- He is perfectly just.
- His mercy endures forever.
- His glory permeates the heavens and the earth.
- He is the source of all beauty.
- He holds the future in His hands.
- He is the King of kings and Lord of lords.

And then we thank God for what he has done:

- He created this magnificent universe.
- He created this beautiful world, perfectly suited to be humanity's home.
- He created human beings from the dust of the earth and breathed life into us.

- He made himself known to us.

- He provides our daily bread from the fruit of the earth.

- He did not abandon us when mankind fell into sin.

- He spoke his Word to us through the Bible, so that we could know who he is, who we are, what our purpose is, what he is doing and is going to do, and how the story of humanity will be resolved.

- He gave us his Law, so that we can know how he designed us to live.

- He chose a people for himself to be his witnesses and special family through whom would come the Messiah.

- And in the fullness of time, he sent Jesus, his only Son, who emptied himself of his prerogative and throne, and came into this world to live and die as one of us.

- Jesus died on the cross for the forgiveness of our sins, and for the salvation of everyone who would believe in Him.

- And he rose again to eternal life, promising those who believe in him that they would live forever in his presence.

- He has adopted those believers as his sons and daughters and made us heirs of his kingdom.

- He invites us into an intimate relationship with him that nothing can destroy.

- Jesus has entrusted to his people the privilege of being his witnesses and taking his love to the world.

- He promised to send the Holy Spirit to empower his disciples to do great things for him.

- He promised he would come again to judge the living and the dead.

- And he promised that at the end of the story, there would be no more sorrow, no more tears, no more pain, no more sin—and the redeemed would dwell with him in joy forever.

If you are a child of God—a believer who has put your trust in Jesus as your Savior, and proclaim him as your Lord (Romans 10:9)—then you have your salvation to thank God for. He has given you faith in him as a gift, and all his promises are for your benefit. And then there are all the blessings God has bestowed personally on you alone.

- The body God has given you;

- Your gifts and talents;

- Your education;

- Your ability to earn a living;

- Your family and friends;

- Your training in the faith;

- The people who have been a blessing in your life;

- The experiences in your life that have made you grow;

- The times God has rescued you from peril;

- The times God has answered your prayers.

To go through such a remarkable list of all God is and all he has done for you is humbling. And it is a source of great joy. Christians commonly have a dramatic encounter with God during such times of praise and thanksgiving. Some have told me that their eyes were opened to how closely God has been walking with them, and that the course they were seeking came readily into focus for them. Some have said that in this prayer time, it became clear they were precisely where God wanted them to be. Others were humbled to recognize that they were children seeking the Father's wisdom, servants seeking the Master's bidding, loved ones seeking to be a blessing to the One they love.

> Shout for joy to the Lord, all the earth.
> Worship the Lord with gladness;
> Come before him with joyful songs.
> Know that the Lord is God.
> It is he who made us, and we are his;
> We are his people, the sheep of his pasture.
> Enter his gates with thanksgiving
> And his courts with praise;
> Give thanks to him and praise his name.
> For the Lord is good and his love endures forever;
> His faithfulness continues through all generations.
> (Psalm 100)

Chapter 4

CONFRONT YOUR SINS

*a*fter King Solomon dedicated the Temple and offered a prayer of consecration over it, God appeared to him at night. God spoke of the times he would send droughts, plagues and swarms of locusts upon the Hebrew people when their sin was great and they needed discipline. And God told Solomon how they could regain his blessing:

> ...if my people, who are called by my name, will humble themselves and pray and seek my face and turn from their wicked ways, I will hear from heaven, and I will forgive their sin and will heal this land. (2 Chronicles 7:14)

We Christians are God's people. We are called by his name. And if we seek his face and expect him to hear, we must humble ourselves, pray for his forgiveness, and turn from our sin. He said elsewhere, "You will seek me and find me if you seek me with all your heart" (Jeremiah 29:13). How can we seek God with all our heart when we are keeping something from him? When we do not confess our sins to him, a part of our heart is withheld from him. Therefore, before asking God to reveal his plan for us, we need to humble ourselves, pray, confess our sins, and turn from our wicked ways.

Charles Colson was a man in the thick of the Watergate Scandal, which brought down the presidency of Richard Milhous Nixon in 1974. Colson was President Nixon's special counsel. Although he maintained that he knew nothing about the White House's illegal scheme to wiretap the offices of the Democratic National Committee, and the subsequent cover-up, Colson went to prison and served seven months of a one-to-three-year term. At the time, he was a brand new Christian. A brilliant man, gifted by God in many ways, Charles Colson wondered how he should serve God now that he was God's man. As he prayed, he confessed and repented:

> In a state of agony, I probed every action I had taken at the White House. There were the tough, ruthless political acts—"dirty tricks"—certainly, because they hurt people. Perhaps even worse in God's eyes there had been arrogance and pride and ego. My all-out loyalty to the Commander-in-Chief had warped and blurred my sense of right and wrong....[5]

Charles Colson believed God had sent him to prison for a reason, and he made a promise to his fellow prisoners to help them. Colson's mission

---

[5]Charles Colson. *Born Again* (Grand Rapids, MI: Chosen Books, Baker Publishing Group, 2008), 217.

became the mobilization of the Christian church to minister to people in prison. In the years he served as founder and chief executive of Prison Fellowship International, Colson went into the darkest places in the United States and foreign countries to take the gospel to desperate incarcerated men. Miraculous stories have emerged of how prison environments in places like Colombia were transformed by God's hand at work through Colson's passionate ministry. Had he not acknowledged his own sin, it is hard to imagine that God would have taken him to such places and use him to such advantage.

We are all sinners. No one's sin is too great for God to forgive. No one is too bad for God to use as an agent for good. But repentance is required of us if we would be God's hands and feet. Charles Colson suffered the ridicule of those who could not take him seriously as a man of God after his notorious transgressions. Most were people who did not understand the power of God's grace. Some were Christians who doubted the sincerity of Colson's conversion. But when they began to see the fruit of his ministry—the changed lives, the people brought to saving faith, the writings of a serious disciple of Jesus Christ—they saw a penitent and forgiven sinner in the service of a generous God. "This is the one I esteem: he who is humble and contrite in spirit, and trembles at my word" (Isaiah 66:2).

Chapter 5

SPIRITUAL DISCIPLINE

Spiritual discipline. To the rebel in us, these words sound too much like work. But to the heart of the believer, they are a warm mantle of joy. For the spiritual disciplines of worship, prayer, Scripture reading and fasting are what enable us to come close to God. Amazingly, the God who made the Pleiades and Orion, who created man from the dust of the earth, who holds the future in his hands, has invited us into intimate communion with him. It is through our worship, prayer, Scripture reading and fasting that we accept that invitation. And it is in that intimacy that we dare say to him, "Teach me your way, Lord. Guide me in the right path. Show me who you would have me be, and what you would have me do." In his Word, written in the Bible, God has already spoken at length about such things. The Bible will lead you toward God's will because, "All scripture is God-breathed and is useful for teaching, rebuking, correcting and training in righteousness, so that the man of God may be thoroughly equipped for every good work" (2 Timothy 3:16-17).

- J.I. Packer, says in *Knowing God* that "...the fundamental mode whereby our rational Creator guides his rational creatures is by rational understanding and application of his written Word."[6]

- A.W.Tozer describes the experience of seeking God's illumination through the Scriptures: "I think that for the average person the progression will be something like this: First a sound as of a presence walking in the garden. Then a voice, more intelligible, but still far from clear. Then the happy moment when the Spirit begins to illuminate the Scriptures, and that which had been only a sound, or at best a voice, now becomes an intelligible word, warm and intimate and clear as the word of a dear friend. Then will come life and light, and best of all, the ability to see and rest in and embrace Jesus Christ as Savior and Lord of all."[7]

> **Reading God's Word is the fundamental way of receiving his guidance.**

- Henry Blackaby recommends a way to pursue the truth revealed in God's Word as a pathway to his purpose for an individual believer's life: "...when God reveals a truth to me in his Word, I write down the passage

---

[6] J.I. Packer. *Knowing God (Downers* Grove, IL: InterVarsity, 1993), 235-6.

[7] A.W. Tozer, *The Pursuit of God* (Abbotsford, WI: Aneko Press, 2015), 66.

of Scripture. Then I meditate on the passage, immersing myself in its meaning. I adjust my life to the truth and thus to God. I agree with God and take any actions necessary to allow God to work in the way he has revealed. Finally, I watch for ways God may use that truth in my life during the day."[8]

READING THE BIBLE

Reading the Bible in a quiet environment with a meditative frame of mind is the foundation for the person seeking to discern God's will, purpose and plan. What do you read? Some will benefit by following whatever program of Bible reading they do as a matter of daily discipline. If your knowledge of Scripture is extensive, you will want to read a passage specifically related to the matter on which you seek God's guidance. Or you might want to read about God speaking to other believers, like Elijah in the cave on Mt. Horeb, or Paul on the road to Damascus, or Samuel in his bed at night, or Moses on Mt. Sinai. You might want to read passages that ignite your love for God in a special way.

Given God's desire to speak to us and the power of the Holy Spirit to illuminate, every encounter with God's Word has the potential to guide us. Whatever your entry point into Scripture, be sure

---

[8] H. and R. Blackaby and C. King, *Experiencing God* (workbook) (Nashville, TN: Lifeway Press, 2007), 105.

to follow up on any threads that come to you. If a verse in the Old Testament reminds you of something in the New Testament, turn to that passage and read it in context. If the name of a person comes up in a reading and you wonder about that person, go to where they are otherwise mentioned. If a word jumps out at you with special force, follow up on its origin, its meaning, and the other places in Scripture where it shows up. Through these and similar connections, God might be leading you.

As you begin to have thoughts about what God might be saying to you, remember that God will never tell you do something that his Word in the Bible condemns. He is the same God yesterday, today, and forever (Hebrews 13:8). Heaven and earth may pass away, but Jesus' words will never pass away (Matthew 24:35). Jesus said, "I tell you the truth, until heaven and earth disappear, not the smallest letter, not the least stroke of a pen, will by any means disappear from the Law until everything is accomplished" (Matthew 5:18).

Draw on the Scriptures that you have committed to memory. I heard a Christmas sermon on the words of Luke that say, "But Mary treasured up all these things, pondering them in her heart" (Luke 2:19). The preacher[9] encouraged us to tuck away God's word in our hearts so that

---

[9] The Rev. Michael Moffitt, Pastor, Light of Christ Anglican Church, Heathsville, Virginia, December 25, 2016 (LightofChristVa.org).

when Satan's lies come, God's truth will rob them of their power over us. The truth of God's Word, memorized, treasured, and pondered over, stands us in good stead when we are struggling to strain out all the messages that can turn our focus away from Jesus.

* * * * *

When Gladys Aylward was a young parlor maid in Britain during the first part of the twentieth century, she gave her life to Christ at a meeting of the Young Life Campaign. Reading one of their magazines, she learned of the Christian missions to China, and she grieved for the millions of Chinese people who had never heard the gospel. God put it in her heart to go to China as a missionary. But how? She failed to get the approval of the China Inland Mission or any other organization. Gladys beseeched God to tell her if the call was real. It was through the Bible that he did so.

Having hardly read the Bible in the past, she began at the beginning. The first story that spoke to her was the story of Abraham. She saw that God had asked him to forsake his home, his people, and his security, and go to a faraway place. That is what she felt God was doing with her. Then she came to the story of Moses and was arrested by the way Moses undertook to obey God and take on the demanding job of leading a difficult people. Again, she saw a servant of God leaving his peaceful, safe hideaway in order to follow the call.

By the time she had read the first two chapters of Nehemiah, she was clear. Nehemiah was a servant to Cyrus, King of Persia, toward the end of the Exile. He had heard of the sad conditions of his fellow Hebrews back in Judah, and he wanted to go there to help. Gladys saw that God had broken Nehemiah's heart for the Hebrews, just as he had broken her heart for the Chinese. Nehemiah had duties to his master, and she had duties to her mistress. After she read Chapter 2, she said, "But he did go, in spite of everything."[10] It was then that she heard God speak in an audible voice, saying, "Gladys Aylward, is Nehemiah's God your God?"

"Yes, of course!" she replied.

"Then do what Nehemiah did, and go."

"But I am not Nehemiah."

"No, but assuredly, I am his God."

That settled everything for her. She believed these were her marching orders.[11] The rest of Gladys Aylward's life story is an amazing chronicle of a small, vulnerable woman acting with obedience and courage, firm in the knowledge that God had revealed to her his plan, and that he would provide everything she needed.

* * * * *

---

[10] Gladys Aylward with Christine Hunter, *The Little Woman* (Chicago: Moody Publishers, 1970), 11.

[11] Gladys Aylward, 11-12

ASKING GOD TO SPEAK

Discerning prayer requires that we ask God to speak to us. We are good at asking God for things. We ask him to give us success in an important meeting. We ask him to heal our loved ones. We ask him to give our friends and family faith to believe in Jesus. We ask him to take us safely to our travel destination, or to bear us up on eagles' wings when the turbulence on our flight becomes alarming. If we are seeking God's will for us, or his plan for our lives, that, too requires prayers of petition. We need to ask him to speak to us.

Don't get me wrong. It is not as if we have to cajole God to communicate with us. We certainly know that God is a communicating God.

> "I am the Lord, and there is no other. I have not spoken in secret from somewhere in a land of darkness," he said. "I have not said to Jacob's descendants, 'Seek me in vain.' " (Isaiah 45:18-19)

God has given us His Word in Holy Scripture to tell us what he wants us to know about the world, about him, about us, about his plan to redeem the world, and about how he wants us to live. He also tells us in the Bible about many encounters he has had with human beings. He spoke to them and gave them assignments. In most cases, they did not ask for those assignments, but God spoke to them anyway. If, however, we are coming to him as he has allowed us to do, and if we have questions we want him to answer about his plans for us, we must ask.

> **God has a broad arsenal of ways to speak to us.**

Perhaps God is waiting for us to give him a sign that we are ready to listen. Or maybe our asking indicates that we will be ready to hear God in whatever way he chooses to speak. As we see in the Bible, God communicates in different ways, not always in audible words.

Speaking Through Visions and Dreams

Sometimes God speaks through an image, as he did to the Apostle Peter when he showed him the "unclean" animals and appointed Peter to take the gospel to the Gentiles (Acts 10:9-16; 11:18). Christians throughout history have experienced visions.

Sometimes God speaks through a dream, as he did to Joseph when he sent an angel to tell him to go ahead and wed Mary, even though she was pregnant (Matthew 1:18-21). Today, visions and dreams given by the Holy Spirit are two of the most prominent ways Muslims are converted to belief in Jesus Christ as the Son of God and Savior of the world. In her book, *Miracle of Miracles,*[12] Mina Nevisa tells about Jesus speaking to her in a

---

[12] Mina Nevisa. *Miracle of Miracles* (Fairfax, VA: Touch of Christ Ministries, 2004), 33.4.

dream when she was a young Muslim in Iran seeking a personal relationship with God. She heard him say, "I am the way, the truth and the life. No one comes to the Father except through me." Soon after, with the help of a friend who was secretly a Christian, she found those words in the Bible. She became a Christian and emigrated to the United States, where today she heads up an organization that ministers to Muslims and offers them the gospel.

Instilling a Burning Desire

Sometimes God gives us a burning desire to do something that we know he wants done. The Rev. E.A. ("Tad") de Bordenave was a parish priest in Richmond, Virginia, when the Lord changed his life dramatically. Tad had taken the "Perspectives Course," a comprehensive look at the history and trajectory of the global Christian mission and the nature of our contemporary evangelistic efforts. In that course, it is shown that the vast majority of modern-day Christian missions are directed at people who were already Christians. Tad was overcome with compassion for the unreached people groups around the globe, among whom there was no Christian presence and no awareness of who Jesus is. He gave up his pastoral ministry and founded Anglican Frontier Missions, whose entire focus is to take the gospel to the twenty least evangelized people groups in the world.

Speaking Through a Sermon

Sometimes the words of a sermon will contain a message specifically for us; this happened to John Wesley on a May evening in 1738 in Aldersgate, as someone read from the preface to Martin Luther's *Epistle to the Romans.*[13] A sermon, preached true to God's Word by a faithful, believing Christian, might stay in someone's memory for many years. And when the time is right, either on the spot or years later, that word will bear fruit.

Messages by Chance Encounter

We must be open to the possibility that a chance encounter with another person may contain the seeds of God's message to us. That is what happened to St. Augustine of Hippo as he sat in his garden. He heard the voice of a child say repeatedly, "Take up and read. Take up and read." Whereupon, Augustine picked up the Bible sitting on his bench, randomly opened it, and read the verses on the opened page. And there he found a message just for him, which brought him to faith and changed his life.[14]

---

[13] Mark Galli and Ted Olsen, *131 Christians Everyone Should Know* (Nashville: Broadman & Holman, 2000), 182.

[14] *The Confessions of St. Augustine* (New York: Image Books, Doubleday, 1960), 202.

The Advice of Mature Christians

Finally, God speaks through his people as they worship, fellowship and minister together in his name. He blesses us with wise believers with whom we have close relationships, people whose wisdom exceeds our own. Asking their thoughts on matters on which you are seeking discernment is always a smart thing to do.

* * * * *

I'm not suggesting that God has a particular fondness for mystery and riddles. However, he certainly has a broad arsenal of ways to speak to us, and some are easier to hear than others.

In October 1995, I went on my first mission trip. It was with a group of five others from SOMA USA, traveling to India to bring a retreat and encouragement to the faculty and students of a missionary college in the interior. In preparation for the trip, we gathered for three days at the home of Edwina Thomas, our team leader. On the third day, I was first out of bed. After my daily Scripture reading, I was very excited. I had read in the Gospel of Luke, Chapter 9, about Jesus sending out his disciples two-by-two into the mission field, and many of the things that happened on that trip were things my prayer team back home had said would happen to us. When our team of six assembled after breakfast, I read this passage from

Luke. Immediately, we were unanimously convicted that God was giving us direction. It was not about what we would do on this trip. Rather, it was about our luggage. Each of us had packed two suitcases, with multiple changes of clothes and plenty of first aid supplies should anything happen to us. As we went and examined our luggage, it looked like a mountain, and we focused on Jesus telling the disciples, "Take nothing for the journey—no staff, no bag, no bread, no money, no extra tunic" (Luke 9:3).

Each of us went back to our room and repacked. We agreed that the women would pack only Indian clothing, and the men would bring only one change of clothes. We would also consolidate our supplies, so that we would have enough for everyone without duplication or excess. And we determined that we would trust God, depend on each other, and receive the hospitable help of our hosts as necessary. We packed only what each of us could fit into one carry-on suitcase for our ten-day trip.

It was an instructive lesson in discernment, for God had a plan. When we got to Mumbai, we were to transfer to another airplane and fly five

> **Test the competing voices that may or may not be God speaking to you.**

hundred miles to Nagpur. But when we got to the ticket counter, we found that an agent had resold our tickets, undoubtedly for a handsome premium. We had no choice but to find another way to Nagpur. We ended up on the third class sleeper train, packed in with about two hundred others in our one car and probably more riding on the roof. All six of us were in one tight, open compartment with bunks stacked three high. Our luggage had to fit with us, chained to the bunks. We marveled at how God had guided us and provided for us by taking away much of the worldly stuff that we thought we needed.

* * * * *

Often our discernment must take on the form of the question, "Was that God who was speaking to me?" This is a question of great significance. If we want to know God's will, we need to strain out the possible competitors: our own inclinations, which are always subject to sinful influences; the devious urging of Satan, whom Jesus called the father of lies (John 8:44); our cultural biases; the wishes of our friends and loved ones; and, especially in the last days, the voices of false prophets (Matthew 24:11).

We must test what we think we have received from God: Is the message consistent with God's Word? Is it rational? Is it consistent with what God is doing in your life? Did it come from the undue influence of a person whose magnetism or ego has swayed your life? Did it come from your own ego and your own sense of self-aggrandizement? Keep your spiritual disciplines in place—redouble them—as you ask these questions.

FASTING

Another spiritual discipline that has helped people seek God's guidance is fasting. Fasting is mentioned often in the Bible, where we see it practiced for mourning, beseeching God in a perilous situation, penitence, and seeking God's guidance.

We are familiar with the term "sack cloth and ashes," which often accompanied fasting, as when David and his soldiers fasted over the death of Saul and Jonathan (2 Samuel 1:12). Nehemiah fasted as he mourned over the sad state of Jerusalem that had been reported to him during the exile (Nehemiah 1:4).

Both in individual and public piety, fasting was used by the Hebrew people to express repentance of their sins. We see the psalmist fasting in repentance in Psalm 69:10. The prophet Joel called for the community to fast over their sins (Joel 1:14). The king of Nineveh called for a citywide fast of repentance after Jonah delivered God's warning of the consequences of their wickedness (Jonah 3:7-9). And the Levitical law required that all Jews fast on the tenth day of the seventh month, the Day of Atonement (Leviticus

16:29).   This is the only mandatory fast in the Bible.

Queen Esther asked the Hebrew people to fast for three days on her behalf, as she prepared to ask King Xerxes to reverse the order to kill all the Hebrews (Esther 4:16). God is not mentioned in this instance (nor is God mentioned anywhere else in the book of Esther). However, the apparent purpose of the fast was to cry out to God on Esther's behalf and ask God's favor on her mission.

The best-known fast in the Bible is Jesus' forty days in the wilderness, where the Holy Spirit sent him immediately after his baptism (Luke 4:1-2). For forty days, Jesus ate nothing. We generally speak of this as preparatory for his ministry, and presume that he was spending that time in intimate communion with the Father, seeking his plan. Another instance is in Acts 13, which reports that the Christian teachers and prophets of Antioch fasted as they worshiped God. Although the Scripture does not tell us why they fasted, it was in response to that worship and fasting that the Holy Spirit said to them, "Set apart for me Barnabas and Saul for the work to which I called them." Acting on this revelation, Saul and Barnabas left for Cyprus to begin spreading the gospel (Acts 13:1-4). Note in the following chapter that Paul (Saul's new name) and Barnabas fasted and prayed over the elders they appointed for the church there (Acts 14:23).

Down through the centuries, many prominent Christians have fasted as a spiritual discipline—people like Martin Luther, John Knox, John Calvin, Jonathan Edwards and John Wesley. In fact, Wesley fasted two days a week and tried unsuccessfully to make that a practice for all his followers. John Calvin, in his *Institutes of Religion,* addressed three purposes of fasting:

> A holy and lawful fast has three ends in view. We use it either to mortify and subdue the flesh, that it may not wanton; or to prepare the better for prayer and holy meditation; or to give evidence of humbling ourselves before God, when we would confess our guilt before him. [15]

"Mortifying and subduing the flesh" takes our mind off the things that distract us from God. As Calvin put it in recalling the fast of the people of Antioch in Acts 13:3, "In general, the only object they had in fasting was to render themselves more alert and disencumbered for prayer."[16] The third purpose, penitently humbling ourselves before God, sets us in proper orientation toward God into whose presence we come as sinners and supplicants.

When the Pharisees asked Jesus why his followers did not fast as they and John the Baptist's disciples did, he spoke of mourning.

---

[15] John Calvin, *Institutes of the Christian Religion,* Book 4, Chapter 12, "15: The Purpose of Fasting."
[16] John Calvin, "16: Fasting and Prayer."

"How can the guests of the bridegroom mourn while he is with them?" he asked. "The time will come when the bridegroom will be taken from them; then they will fast" (Matthew 9:14-15).

Indeed, there is much to mourn as we contemplate the separation between us and God that came about through the sin of Adam. Adam and Eve, before the Fall, had a natural closeness with God, and they communicated with him as they enjoyed his presence in the garden. We mourn over the tragedy that human sin has so profoundly damaged that intimacy. Fasting is an entirely appropriate response as we humble ourselves before God and seek his guidance.

Historically, only a minority of American Christians have practiced fasting as a regular spiritual discipline. In recent times, however, people are rediscovering the efficacy of fasting when seeking God's face. Much useful advice has been written about proper and improper ways to fast. A good resource on the subject is Richard Foster's book, *Celebration of Discipline, The Path to Spiritual Growth*.[17] Jesus told us that "...man does not live by bread alone but by every word that comes from the mouth of God" (Matthew 4:4). Fasting reminds us of this. It shows us that it is not essential for us to eat three times a day. And many Christians report that fasting enhances their

---

[17] Richard Foster, *Celebration of Discipline: The Path to Spiritual Growth* (San Francisco: Harper, Revised Edition 1988), Chapter 4.

ability to listen to God, for their sense of spiritual hearing intensifies. As the Bible tells us pointedly, it is not God who has moved away from us, but we who have moved away from God (Isaiah 59:1-2).

*   *   *   *   *

> **The key is to give God your undivided attention.**

In my third year out of seminary, I accepted my first position as pastor of a congregation. I was to move there at the beginning of July. After Easter, I went on a retreat to seek God's guidance for my new ministry. I went away to a quiet place. I left behind all distractions. I tried to quiet my mind. The second night, I heard what seemed to be an audible voice, which said simply, "Love them." If I had been in any other environment, I would have thought my own mind had thrown out those words. My reaction would have been, "Well, of course I should love them. That's what the Bible tells me. I need more guidance than that." But, because I had surrendered to a quiet mind, and had done so with purpose, I knew God had spoken to me. And I knew he was not just saying, "Do what my Word tells you." He was speaking to me in the deep places. I was convicted that he was telling me I had work to do concerning love. I was capable of detachment that would not serve me well in pastoral ministry. And I knew also that he was telling me to love the people under my care in a way that would enable them to feel God's love.

On the tenth anniversary of my ministry at that congregation, there was a dinner to mark the occasion. One of the gifts I received was a scrap book with pictures and letters from members of the congregation. A theme that came through in what the people said in their notes was that they were thankful for the way I loved them, and that they could feel God's love through their pastor. God had indeed spoken to me ten years earlier.

There is no set formula for successfully seeking God's voice. But Jesus said, "Seek and you shall find, knock and the door shall be opened to you" (Matthew 7:7). The key is to seek him conscientiously, wanting to hear from him and setting aside those things that prevent our hearing his voice. The key is to give God your undivided attention.

Waiting for God's guidance may take some time:

> 'Wait on the Lord' is a constant refrain in the Psalms, and it is a necessary word, for God often keeps us waiting. He is not in as much hurry as we are, and it is not his way to give more light on the future than we need for action in the present—or to guide us more than one step at a time."[18]

---

[18] J.I. Packer. *Knowing God (Downers* Grove, IL: InterVarsity, 1993), 235-6.

With the Lord, a day is like a thousand years, (2 Peter 3:8) and it may seem to us that God is slow in speaking. As we wait for God to give us clear direction, we should keep asking. Develop and maintain the spiritual disciplines that you put in place at the beginning of your discernment campaign. Continue to march in Christ's footsteps, being his witness and loving God with your whole heart, mind, soul and strength—and loving your neighbor as yourself. Strengthen your efforts to live a holy life. Our line of communication with God becomes strangely filled with static when we are living in ways that are offensive to him. However, when we are living Christ-like lives, the static begins to clear. Hear the words of 1 Peter:

> Therefore, prepare your minds for action; be self-controlled, set your hope fully on the grace to be given you when Jesus Christ is revealed. As obedient children, do not conform to the evil desires you had when you lived in ignorance. But just as he who called you is holy, so be holy in all you do; for it is written: "Be holy, because I am holy." (1 Peter 1:13-16)

Chapter 6

ASK GOD TO OPEN YOU TO THE HOLY SPIRIT

*a*s we seek to discern God's plan and then surrender ourselves to that plan, we will need at every stage to ask God to open us to his Holy Spirit. We will need the Holy Spirit to reveal God's plan to us. We will need the Holy Spirit as we seek to be obedient in the role he reveals to us. And as we move into that ministry, we will need the Holy Spirit's continuing guidance and power to accomplish God's will.

Being open to the Holy Spirit is being willing to allow him to move freely in us and in the things we do. That entails that we trust him as he operates beyond the knowledge and wisdom we ourselves possess, and beyond our own power to make things happen. It is a given that the Holy Spirit is already dwelling in us. Jesus promised that he would send the Holy Spirit to dwell in us (John 14:15-16).

In fact, Jesus told the disciples he would have to leave them so that the Holy Spirit could come (John 16:7). But we can resist him by our fear, our sin and disbelief. The Spirit of God came upon King Saul when he began his reign (1 Samuel 10:10), but Saul was repeatedly disobedient to God, and the Holy Spirit departed from him (1 Samuel 16:14). The first letter to the Thessalonians warns us not to quench the Spirit (1 Thessalonians 5:19), suggesting that as rain puts out a wildfire, our own unfaithful actions can douse the flames of the Holy Spirit's work in us.[19]

On the other hand, when we are open to the Holy Spirit working in us, letting him do as he will, Scripture tells us that he can do immeasurably more than we can ask or imagine (Ephesians 3:20). Recall that Jesus said we would do greater things than he (John 14:12). He said that whatever we ask in his name he would give us (John 16:23).

> **The work of the Holy Spirit is to manifest the active presence of God in the world.**

Much has been said and taught about what the Holy Spirit does. A helpful definition of his role is captured in Wayne Grudem's *Systematic Theology*, where he says:

> The work of the Holy Spirit is to manifest the active presence of God in the world, and especially in the Church.[20]

---

[19] Ephesians 4:30 uses the term "grieve" the Holy Spirit. The context suggests we do this by our sin.

[20] Wayne Grudem, *Systematic Theology* (Grand Rapids MI: Zondervan, 1994), 634.

When you are filled with the Holy Spirit, Grudem asserts, you are: "…feeling what God feels, desiring what God desires, doing what God wants, speaking by God's power, praying and ministering in God's strength, and knowing with the knowledge that God Himself gives."[21]

A. W. Tozer, in his classic work, *Mystery of the Holy Spirit*, identifies seven ways believers are transformed when they are filled with the Holy Spirit:[22]

- They have a sudden brilliant consciousness of God being actually present.

- They have the joy of the Holy Ghost, a "post-resurrection" joy.

- Their words have the power to penetrate and arrest.

- They possess a clear sense of the reality of everything.

- There is a sharp separation between them and the world.

- They take great delight in prayer.

- They have a passionate love for the Scriptures.

From the time of the Book of Acts down to today, Christians have been involved in startling

---

[21] Wayne Grudem, 648-9

[22] A.W. Tozer, *Mystery of the Holy Spirit* (Alachua, FL: Bridge-Logos, 2007), 55-62.

works of God as they experienced these manifestations of the Holy Spirit. Those who unexpectedly found themselves leading a major revival have been amazed by the work of the Holy Spirit. Those who have stumbled in prayer have found the Holy Spirit doing their praying for them (Romans 8:26). Those who have given what they thought was a pedestrian sermon have found that the Holy Spirit brought conviction and conversion to their listeners. Christians have found themselves suddenly in deep grief over the things around them that break the heart of God. Those who have gone out on a limb, trusting the Holy Spirit, have been astounded by the miracles he has done through prayer and laying on of hands.

Jesus promised that the Holy Spirit would guide us into all truth (John 16:13). He said that the Holy Spirit would remind us of everything Jesus taught us (John 14:26). Paul said in Ephesians 1:17-19 that he would give us understanding. And in the Acts of the Apostles, we see these things coming to pass:

> **The Holy Spirit will guide us into God's plan for us if we open our hearts to him.**

- Philip was told to look for a certain Ethiopian man, whom God was going to convert (Acts 8:29).

- Peter was given a vision and an insight, and then sent by the Holy Spirit to the home of Cornelius the Centurion, where the entire family became Christians and were baptized (Acts 10:19-20).

- At Antioch, the Holy Spirit revealed to the believers that he had set Paul and Barnabas apart for certain missionary work (Acts 13:2).

- The apostles testified that the Holy Spirit guided them at the Council of Jerusalem as to what to tell the Gentile converts about the burden of Jewish ritual requirements (Acts 15:28).

- Acts 16:6-7 tells us that the Holy Spirit prevented Paul from going to the province of Asia to preach.

The Bible gives us many glimpses of the work of the Holy Spirit, all of which encourage us that he will guide us into God's plan for us if we open our hearts to Him.

> **Holiness of life is a bulwark of the Christian seeking to know and follow God's plan.**

We also find in the epistles that the Holy Spirit works to make us holy. Peter told the Church, "Live holy lives as you look forward to Jesus' coming again so that you may advance that day" (2 Peter 3:11-14). Our holiness actually can advance the Lord's return! What does *holy* mean? *Holy* means "set apart for God." When we speak of God's holiness, we are referring to an attribute of his being. He is unique. By his very being, he is set apart from everything else, for everything else is his creation.

When we speak of the holiness of human beings, we inevitably think of goodness and righteousness, qualities that God can confer on us to make us like him. The first letter to the Corinthians says it is the Holy Spirit who "sanctifies" us—i.e., makes us holy (1 Corinthians 6:11). The Bible also says that the Holy Spirit is transforming us into the likeness of Christ (2 Corinthians 3:17-18). Romans 8:29 tells us that, "Those whom God foreknew, he also destined to be conformed to the likeness of his Son, that he might be the firstborn among many brothers."

Holiness of life means living in a Christ-like manner. God calls us to be holy so that we may be closer to him. And as we walk intimately with him, we will find that people are attracted when they see godliness in us. If they fail to see a difference between us and everyone else in the world, our credibility is diminished. Simply deciding to be a better person is not going to make us so. We do not have it in us to defeat our sin. That is the work of the Holy Spirit. And the more the fruits of the Spirit are manifest in us—love, joy, peace, patience, kindness, goodness, faithfulness, gentleness and self-control (Galatians 5:22-25)— the more like Jesus we are.

Holiness of life is a bulwark of the Christian seeking to know and follow God's plan. As previously discussed, holiness is essential to maintaining an unobstructed communication channel with God. It keeps us free from wanting things that are not the things of God, thus enhancing our ability to distinguish God's voice from the other voices vying for our attention. In our ministry, holiness of

> **As we move into our ministry as part of God's plan, the importance of our openness to the Holy Spirit continues.**

life makes it possible to maintain our credibility with those whom we seek to influence with the life-transforming gospel.

The power of God's Word to transform lives is the work of the Holy Spirit. He prepares the hearts of people to hear and respond to the gospel. Jesus said the Holy Spirit will convict the world of guilt with regard to sin and righteousness and judgment (John 16:7-11). And we know that he also speaks through the faithful preaching of the gospel. When Peter and John came before the Sanhedrin to answer for healing the man at the gate called "Beautiful," Peter was filled with the Holy Spirit and preached boldly and with courage (Acts 4:8 and 4:31). Paul testified to the Thessalonians that he had brought the gospel to them with the power of the Holy Spirit (1 Thessalonians 1:5).

Over the centuries, there have been great revivals when the Holy Spirit has been in the preaching and has made a sovereign choice to minister to the crowds. The Moravian Revival in

Germany (1727), the Great Awakening in New England (1730's and 40's), the Welsh Revival (1904-05), the Azusa Street Revival in California beginning in 1906, and the East African Revival (1920's and 30's) have had dramatic and enduring effects on the Church and the world. The hand of the Holy Spirit is obvious in all of them. One of the key figures of the Great Awakening was Jonathan Edwards, whose preaching sparked a revival in Northampton, Massachusetts, at the church where he served.[23] And yet, it was not theatrics or the force of his personality that brought such fruit of salvation. Someone who saw Jonathan Edwards preach said of him:

> He scarcely gestured or even moved, and he made no attempt by the elegance of his style or the beauty of his pictures to gratify the taste and fascinate the imagination.[24]

Clearly, the Holy Spirit was at work in the faithful preaching of Jonathan Edwards.

It is easy to identify such moments, events and movements as miraculous. The hand of God intervenes to take our meager efforts and bring conviction, confession, belief and redemption. Often, in partnership with a disciple yielded to the

---

[23] Jonathan Edwards wrote a contemporaneous account of this remarkable revival, entitled, *An American Revival: An Account of a Surprising Move of God* (Goodyear, AZ: Diggory Press, 2007).
[24] Quoted in "131 Christians Everyone Should Know," *Christian History Magazine,* (Nashville: Broadman & Holman, 2000), 182.

Holy Spirit, God will perform a miracle to display his power so that those who witness it may know that he is God and stand humbly before him. Such was the case, according to the book of Judges, when God dealt with Gideon. He plied Gideon from the winepress where he was

> **God performs miracles to display his power so that those who witness them will know that he is God.**

cowering in fear of the Midianites. God gave him the enormous job of leading soldiers in battle against the dreaded enemy. And then he directed Gideon to whittle down the number of his troops from thirty-two thousand to three hundred. Forcing them to face an army that vastly outnumbered them, and of whom they were very much afraid, God told Gideon that his purpose in reducing the army to three hundred was "...in order that Israel may not boast against me that her own strength has saved her" (Judges 7:2).

In the same way today, God heals, raises the dead, sweeps away barriers, restores relationships—sometimes to humble us with his power, and sometimes to empower the ministry of an obedient servant who has called on the Holy Spirit.

Another thing the Holy Spirit does in our ministry is to endow us with spiritual gifts— abilities and offices that God uses to accomplish his plan of redemption through the obedience of his people.

The Holy Spirit gives us spiritual gifts to empower us to do his work.

Paul spoke of this in 1 Corinthians 12:7: "Now to each one the manifestation of the Spirit is given for the common good." The common good must be seen in the context of our ministry to be Christ's witnesses and purvey his love. When Paul speaks of spiritual gifts in Ephesians 4:7-16, he points to offices, such as pastor, teacher and evangelist. He tells us the gifts are given "to prepare God's people for works of service...." (Ephesians 4:12).

When we come before governors and kings, we do not stand there on our own.

There is one more function of the Holy Spirit that Jesus promised us. He said that when we come into conflict with those in authority because of our commitment to stand fast for the gospel, the Holy Spirit will give us the words we need to speak (Luke 12:12, Matthew 10:20). We will not stand there on our own. The Holy Spirit will transform our ordeal of interrogation and accusation into occasions to testify persuasively of the saving love of Jesus. If we come to such a point, this promise will be most reassuring. But it will take great faith and submission to the Holy Spirit to trust our defense to God.

Most Christians would recognize that the work of discerning God's plan for them will require turning to the Holy Spirit, revealer of truth and understanding. It is perhaps less obvious that discerning the plan without continuing to open ourselves to the Holy Spirit will be an exercise of small consequence. If, however, we continuously yield to the Holy Spirit as an ongoing orientation, God's plan will shine in us like the brightness of the sun.

Chapter 7

CORPORATE DISCERNMENT

So far, we have looked at discerning God's plan as a matter of personal faith and practice. There is a wider dimension of which individual discernment is a part. It is healthy and often essential for entire congregations to engage in discernment. What is God's will for us as his people, whom he has brought together for a purpose? We like to think that we have joined a congregation because we have chosen it, based on objective criteria: the biblical preaching, the style of the liturgy, the hospitality of the members, the beauty of the worship facility, the good nursery, the excellent choir, the nature of the ministries. Our choosing is, without question, a piece of the puzzle of how we happen to be members of our congregation. But there is a larger reality: God has brought us there. And he has brought the other members there, because he has a plan and a purpose for them. Sadly, many congregations miss God's plan because they are too focused on their own biases, preferences and experiences. Even when a congregation is clicking along, plainly doing God's work, it is   important to reevaluate from time to time whether God has a new focus for them.

Since the advent of modern democracy in the eighteenth century, most Western institutions, including the churches, have adopted the majority vote as a way of expressing the will of the people who have stakes in those institutions. But is the will of the members the right benchmark for a church? What they should seek to discover is God's will, God's plan, God's purpose. Therefore, there needs to be a vehicle for congregational discernment that leads up to the voting, so that the members' votes reflect God's will, rather than their own.

Between 2003 and 2016, the congregation I served as pastor went through a turbulent time. Life at St. Stephen's Episcopal Church was peaceful and harmonious until it was shaken by the decision of the Episcopal Church to consecrate a partnered homosexual as the Bishop of New Hampshire. Some of our members welcomed that decision as part of an inevitable modernization of the church. For most in our congregation, however, this decision was a radical departure from the demands of Scripture. For the first three years, we watched as the international Anglican hierarchy made moves as if to discipline the Episcopal Church and peel back its new doctrine. But in 2006, the national church passed resolutions to further solidify its unbiblical stance. Along with about a dozen congregations in our

Episcopal diocese, St. Stephen's undertook a forty-day period of discernment in preparation for congregational votes on whether to disaffiliate from the Episcopal Church.

Our discernment period had several components. Each Sunday, there was a sermon on an aspect of the question, followed by a congregational forum. The forums focused on questions ranging from what the Bible says about homosexuality, to the New Testament's pervasive emphasis on the dangers of false teaching, to what the costs would be if we voted to leave the Episcopal Church.

There were seven small group venues during the week, and the members were asked to attend at least one. Each gathering included discerning prayer, and the members were encouraged to fast and pray on their own over the question of disaffiliation. It was a time of uncommon openness among our members about their beliefs, fears and expectations. Some of the small group sessions and forums were heated, as they should have been, given the gravity of the subject matter.

The forty-day period ended a week before the congregation voted. The vote was seventy-five percent in favor of leaving the Episcopal Church, and we embarked on a journey through uncharted waters. We endured five years of litigation, loss of friendships, and loss of our buildings, furnishings and supplies, along with several hundred thousand dollars in bank balances. We spent three years housed in the facilities of a Baptist congregation that generously took us in. Between 2012 and 2015, we convened other discernment periods to deal with questions of our corporate life:

- What will our new vision and ministries be?

- Should we build a church, and if so, what should it be like in character and scope

- What should the name of our congregation be?

These were all decisions that would be made by the vestry, the elected leadership of the congregation in Anglican polity. The discernment periods were aimed at equipping members to speak their mind faithfully at congregational meetings as input to the vestry's discernment process. By November 2015, we were worshiping in a new church facility and our name had been changed to "Light of Christ Anglican Church."

The appendix in this book consists of Scripture readings and meditations that we distributed for a discernment period of four weeks in October and November of 2014. The focus of these readings is "Hearing from God." Thus, these materials may be useful for any congregation's corporate discernment, regardless of what the presenting issues may be.

I find it difficult to visualize how complex and potentially divisive all this decision-making would have been without the concerted effort to come together and seek God's plan, purpose and will for us. Not only did it put us on the right track, but it also made us a peaceful and unified congregation, eager to be Jesus' disciples.

Chapter 8

ASK GOD FOR WISDOM ON HOW TO PROCEED

*a*s God begins to reveal his plan to you, there is still a long way to go. It is a wonderful thing to have clarity and peace on how God wants to deploy you. But now what? You can be confident God is not going to leave you high and dry. It is his plan and he promises, "… my word that goes out from my mouth: It will not return to me empty, but will accomplish what I desire and achieve the purpose for which I sent it" (Isaiah 55:11). Does that mean, then, that you just sit back and watch? That is not what we see in the Bible when God calls people to serve him.

He is a God who expects something of the people he has saved. That is part of the joy of being a disciple: Your days are filled with faithful acts performed in concert with the Maker of heaven and earth. What could be more fulfilling? What could be more exciting? Paul said in his letter to the Philippians, "I want to know Christ and the power of his resurrection and the fellowship of sharing in his sufferings, becoming like him in his death…." (Philippians 3:10). He embraced the joy of identifying with Jesus, even when it meant hardship and suffering.

If Jesus wanted to do his work with only our token involvement, why would he tell us so much about how he wants us to live? Why would he press upon us the Greatest and the Second Great Commandment? Why would he tell us we should be holy because the Lord our God is holy? Why would he spend three years training his disciples? Because he wants us to be actively engaged. That raises important questions: How do we begin? Where do we go from here? This should become the focus of our prayers at this stage of discovering and pursuing God's plan for us. We need to ask God for wisdom to know our next step.

If God is calling you to bring his love and compassion to people in the last days of life, or homeless people, or people in prison:

- How do you get educated about what they are going through?

- How do you connect with a group of people engaged in this work?

- Should you attempt to persuade a secular agency to allow you to bring faith into their work through your ministry?

- Should you work through your congregation?

- Should this be full-time or part-time?

- How will you make a living as you pursue this ministry?

If God is calling you to bring the gospel to people of other faiths:

- Who are the people to whom he is calling you?

- Who can teach you what those people believe and hold dear?

- Where can you get the language skills you will need?

- How do you make connections that will get you there?

- How will you go about raising money for your mission work?

- Should this be a series of short-term missions or a life-long move?

- How will you fulfill your responsibilities to your family?

If God's plan is that you work in the secular world and exhibit his saving grace to co-workers, clients and strangers:

- Where should you go to school?

- What career or job should you take?

- Where should you live?

- How can you learn more about personal evangelism?

- What congregation should be your base of operations?

- How equipped is your family to support you enthusiastically in this lifestyle?

- What sacrifices are they prepared to make?

- What teaching do you need to share with them?

These are all simply examples of the questions that you would need to address. You will discover many more. It is at this point that you can easily become overwhelmed and get bogged down. And this is when you should remind yourself that you and God are partners in his plan. God will expect you to ask him to continue guiding you and to show you what the next moves should be. God will take joy in that; his intent is that you will take joy in it too, for you are partnering with the One you love. God seeks that continuing intimacy with you. Jesus said:

> Ask and it will be given to you; seek and you will find; knock and the door will be opened to you. For everyone who asks receives; he who seeks finds; and to him who knocks, the door will be opened. Which of you, if his son asks for bread, will give him a stone? Or if he asks for a fish, will give him a snake? If you, then, though you are evil, know how to give good gifts to your children, how much more will your Father in heaven give good gifts to those who ask him! (Matthew 7:7-11)

It is easy to make a common mistake at this point: doing nothing until God has laid out in detail all the steps needed to make this a successful ministry or mission. He is a God of action, and when he speaks, his disciples should be ready for action. Often that will mean taking some uncomfortable first steps when we have only part of the picture. Knowing when to take those first steps and when to hold back a little for further discernment is something his disciples have to figure out for themselves, trusting in him who will never leave us or forsake us (Joshua 1:5).

Peter Marshall was a boy in Scotland early in the twentieth century.[25] He lived in the industrial town of Coatbridge near Glasgow with his mother and stepfather. He had an obsessive desire to go to sea and repeatedly got in trouble for trying to stow away on ships in the harbor. Even after Peter promised his mother he would not stow away again, something kept pulling at him from beyond the sea.

One night, as he prayed fervently for guidance, the Lord told him his plan was for Peter to be a preacher. Not knowing what to do next, Peter stayed in Coatbridge working at the local mill until he raised enough money to book passage to America. Once in America, again, he worked as a laborer, and continued to ask God what he should do next. In Birmingham, Alabama, where a friend had urged him to move, Peter became involved in a Presbyterian church, and there, the members of

---

[25] See biography, written by his wife: Catherine Marshall, *A Man Called Peter* (New York: McGraw Hill, 1951).

his Sunday School class raised the money for him to attend seminary in Atlanta. He excelled as a student and was highly sought after upon graduation.

Always, he continued to ask for God's wisdom when decisions were to be made. When the New York Avenue Presbyterian Church in Washington, D.C., pursued Marshall to be their pastor, he turned them down. He was intimidated by this pulpit, where pastors had preached to U.S. presidents from Abraham Lincoln forward. He said he was too immature, too inexperienced, and not sure he would ever be ready for that pastorate. However, they continued to pursue him, and in his prayers, he eventually sensed God was calling him there. He served there from 1937 until his untimely death in 1949, having brought that church from a declining, self-important congregation, to one with overflowing crowds on Sundays and many compassion ministries. During his tenure there, Marshall was twice appointed Chaplain to the U.S. Senate, where he was greatly loved for his humility and pointed prayers.

This man had a huge impact on policymakers during a pivotal time in American history. If he had not asked God to reveal his plan, would he have ended up as a sailor? Or if he had not persistently sought God's guidance, would his fear of the New York Avenue church pulpit have kept him from preaching to presidents and senators?

God's plans cannot be thwarted, of course. But oh, the beauty of a life given over to God and lived according to God's wisdom!

Chapter 9

Ask God for Obedience

God's plan for redeeming the world includes working through his faithful servants—you and me. Sometimes he uses us without our conscious cooperation. Sometimes he works through us without our knowledge. I know a dozen different stories, including one of my own, of Christians bringing someone to faith in Jesus but not knowing it until much later when they encountered that person by accident and learned what had happened. When we hear such things, we rejoice and humbly thank God for using us.

On the other hand, when God reveals a plan for us, we might not rejoice. We sometimes resist. We may find the timing inconvenient, as when Jesus told people to follow him, and they said such things as, "Let me go back and bury my father," or "Let me say goodbye to my family" (Luke 9:57-62). We may protest that we aren't up to the task, as Moses did. God had to convince him by insisting that he had indeed chosen Moses, and that's how it was going to be. We may resist because we are afraid, or because we can't see the pathway to success, or for any number of reasons.

I am not at all suggesting that God's plans for us are cruel tasks that require us to do things we hate. But I am pointing out the human tendency to object, procrastinate and float along on the inertia of the familiar in our lives. Read the lives of the great Christians of the past. It is rare to find one who didn't negotiate with God over his plan. At such times we have a need for a God-given quality that we call *obedience.* We tend to look at obedience as our human effort to do what God commands. But as disciples of Jesus, who saved us by grace through faith, it makes more sense to think of obedience as a gift from God that enables us to overcome our reticence to do and be what God calls us to do and be.

> **Obedience is a gift from God that enables us to overcome our reticence to do and be what God calls us to do and be.**

From this perspective, a part of discerning God's plan for us is to ask that he enable us to be obedient. We can begin praying for obedience at the very beginning of our discernment process: "Lord, show me your plan for me, and enable me to embrace it and do as you ask of me." Equally, we will need to pray for obedience once we have some inkling of his plan and a sense of his desire that we follow a certain path.

Perhaps a definition of obedience in this context would help. God's interaction with

Abraham suggests that obedience is the action that comes from trusting God to provide, protect and fulfill. "Abram believed God, and it was credited to him as righteousness" (Genesis 15:6). God told Abram to go to a land that God would show him. And what would happen as a result, God said, was that Abram would have a multitude of descendants, even though he was a childless old man and his elderly wife was barren. Moreover, the entire world would be blessed by his descendants.

With nothing but this to go on, Abram (now renamed "Abraham" by God) went west until God told him to stop. His wife bore him the son God had promised, and Abraham saw in that son the hopes for the posterity God had promised. And yet, a few years later, God tested Abraham and told him to go to a mountaintop and sacrifice this son Isaac. Abraham went as God had told him. The Bible does not tell us what was in Abraham's mind, but it does show him with the knife poised above his son. And then God provided, in Isaac's place, a ram for the offering. This obedience by God's servant Abraham was extreme. It is, in fact, superhuman. Just as God had given a son to an old man and his barren wife, and just as God had provided the ram, God provided the trust that enabled Abraham to know that all God's promises were true, despite the appearances.

This God, who called and tested and empowered Abraham, has a plan for each of his faithful servants. Once the servant has discerned God's plan, he would do well to pray something like this:

> God, you have given me a glimpse of what you want me to do. Now, make me obedient to you. Please give me the ability to trust you completely. Empower me to act as you call me to act, knowing that you will provide everything I need, protect me from the world, the flesh and the devil, and bring fruit that will advance your Kingdom as you see fit.

A.W. Tozer, in his book, *God's Pursuit of Man*, speaks of God's will and man's will as two separate worlds.

> There are two worlds, set over against each other, dominated by two wills: the will of man and the will of God, respectively. The old world of fallen nature is the world of human will. There man is king and his will decides events. So far as he is able in his weakness he decides who and what and when and where.[26]

We love to say, "I have decided," and think we have the freedom and the power to control our destiny. But above human will is the other world, which Tozer calls "the world of God's sovereign will where the will of man cannot come, or if it comes, it is as

---

[26] A.W. Tozer, *God's Pursuit of Man* (Chicago: Moody Publishers, 2015), 46.

a dependent and a servant, never as lord."[27] Coming into God's will as a servant is called obedience.

Jesus said, "If you obey my commands, you will remain in my love" (John 15:10). On the one hand, this statement emphasizes our relationship as creatures to the God who created us. If we love him, then, as his creatures, our required response is to *obey* him. And yet, there is more here, and Jesus' choice of words is perplexing, for it would not be like Jesus to say, "I will love you as long as you keep my Law." Romans 8:39 tells us that nothing in all creation can separate us from the love of God that is in Christ Jesus. More likely, Jesus was saying something like this: "Play the role I have assigned to you, and you will continue to work with me in the plan of redemption for which, in my love, I gave my life on the cross." Jesus is defining what our response should be as his followers; setting the priorities he demands will bring us into immense blessing. He told the disciples, "You did not choose me, but I chose you and appointed you to bear fruit—fruit that will last" (John 15:16). Jesus has a plan for each of us, his disciples. And for as long as we are walking in that plan, it is our privilege to bear fruit that will advance his comprehensive plan of redeeming the whole world.

---

[27] A.W. Tozer, 45.

From this perspective, we can see obedience as a gift from God. The gift of obedience frees us from the tyranny of our own preferences, priorities, biases, assumptions, fears, commitments and attractions. With that kind of freedom, we are able to do as God says, right down to the small details. And we never know which small details are critical to God's plan. He sees the big picture, the whole picture. We see as though through a glass darkly, for now we see only a part (1 Corinthians 13:12). But one day, we will see God face to face; imagine the joy when we see those small acts of obedience that turned out to have huge significance.

Jim Cymbala, pastor of the Brooklyn Tabernacle, tells the story of a long night in Indianapolis, when he bowed obediently to God's will. It was the night before he was to address a convention on church music attended by ten thousand Christians.[28] From past experience, he knew this group came mostly to hear gospel music, and so he had been leaning toward preaching a "simple message of encouragement." The night before his address, he prayed for God's guidance as to what to preach, and God insistently pushed him toward a message he had preached not long before on "My house will be called a house of prayer" (Mark 11:17). "It's a very direct message," says Cymbala. "It deals with Jesus' cleaning the

---

[28] Jim Cymbala, *Fresh Power* (Grand Rapids, MI: Zondervan, 2003), 9-15.

merchants out of the temple and pointedly calls the audience to what the church is really for, as opposed to all the misuses we make of it." Wrestling with the thought of this for several hours, and the reaction he might get from the audience and the organizers, Cymbala nevertheless went to bed determined to be obedient. The next day, he preached that pointed message. That sermon had great impact there at the convention. And for several years thereafter, Cymbala received requests to speak at Christian gatherings. He also received many letters telling him of the impact the video of that sermon was having on Christians around the country.

I will talk in the next chapter about the courage Christ's disciples need to follow his plan. But first, a brief admonition not to be anxious about whether our obedience is precisely correct or even adequate. Remember, we are saved by grace. In fact, being obedient to God ought to chase away our stress. For we need not strive desperately for success. It is God's plan, and God will bring the fruit. We are simply his servants, doing as he instructs. God has spelled it out for us in Scripture: "Be still and know that I am God" (Psalm 46:10).

Chapter 10

ASK GOD FOR COURAGE

*a*nyone who seeks God's plan with the intent to follow it is going to need a character trait that not all of us naturally possess. That trait is *courage*. It takes courage even to ask God what his plan is for your life. For once he tells you, you will never again be at peace until you are following his track. As I said at the outset, you may be reluctant to give up control over your own plans—or should I say, you may not want to give up the illusion that you have control over your own life. The letter of James tells us it is foolish and arrogant to say what we are going to do tomorrow, for we will do only what God wills or permits (James 4:13-15). Jesus told the parable about a farmer who had an abundant crop; he planned to tear down his barns and build bigger ones to store the excess. His plan was to put his feet up and eat, drink and be merry. But God said to the man:

> You fool! This very night your life will be demanded from you. Then who will get what you have prepared for yourself?" (Luke 12:20)

So God's wisdom tells us that our lives are in his hands, and "giving over control to Him" ought not to require courage. Still, it is frightening for us to wait for what God may tell us he expects us to do, largely because we don't think expansively enough about what we are capable of doing in his strength.

For that very reason, it also requires courage to embark on whatever mission God sends us on. If it were easy, we wouldn't need to pray for obedience. Beyond what we think we are capable of accomplishing, we are not certain of our ability to endure suffering. We know that hardship will accompany God's plan. How could it be otherwise? God is redeeming a world that denies it needs to be redeemed. The world is in the thrall of a clever and persuasive enemy, the fallen angel whom the Bible calls Satan, the evil one, the destroyer, the deceiver. He puts his most forceful efforts to work against those who faithfully answer God's call, for he knows God's

> *In each instance when Jesus warned us of the pain, he gave us a promise to encourage us.*

power will be at work in such people. And we know to expect Satan to come against us. Jesus was clear on that, and he reminded his disciples of it repeatedly.

- In the Sermon on the Mount, he told us people would insult us, persecute us, and falsely say all kinds of evil against us because of him (Mathew 5:11).

- Another time, he said, "All men will hate you because of me...." (Matthew 10:22)

- When he spoke of the last days, Jesus said, "You will be betrayed even by parents, brothers, relatives and friends, and they will put some of you to death" (Luke 21:16).

- When he prayed for his disciples the night of the Last Supper, Jesus said, "I have given them your word and the world has hated them, for they are not of the world, any more than I am of the world. My prayer is not that you would take them out of the world but that you protect them from the evil one" (John 17:14-15).

Being hated, betrayed, insulted, persecuted and lied about are painful things. There is no shame in fearing such injuries. Therefore, asking God for courage is necessary to keep us underway and on track as his disciples. Inevitably, he will remind us that in each instance when he warned us of the pain, he gave us a promise to encourage us:

- Blessed are you, for yours is the Kingdom of Heaven (Matthew 5:10).

- Those who stand firm to the end will be saved (Matthew 10:22).

- "But not a hair on your head will perish. By standing firm, you will gain life" (Luke 21:18-19).

- "I have told you these things so that you may have peace. In this world you will have trouble. But take heart! I have overcome the world" (John 16:33).

Martin Luther King was not immune to fear. It took great courage for him to continue in the leadership role God had assigned to him in the face of threats, physical attacks, and even opposition by some of the people he expected to count as allies. In a sermon entitled, "Our God is Able," he told the story of the threats he received in 1958 to bomb his house.

> Almost immediately after the Montgomery bus protest had been undertaken, we began to receive threatening telephone calls and letters in our home. Sporadic in the beginning, they increased day after day. At first, I took them in stride, feeling that they were the work of a few hotheads, who would become discouraged after they discovered that we would not fight back. But as the weeks passed, I realized that the threats were in earnest. I felt myself faltering and growing in fear.
>
> After a particularly strenuous day, I settled in bed at a late hour. My wife had already fallen asleep and I was about to doze off when the telephone rang. An angry voice said, "Listen, nigger, we've taken all we want from you. Before next week, you'll be sorry you ever came to Montgomery." I hung up, but I could not sleep. It seemed that all of my fears had come down on me at once. I had reached the saturation point.
>
> I got out of bed and began to walk the floor. Finally, I went to the kitchen and heated a pot of coffee. I was ready to give up. I tried to think

of a way to move out of the picture without appearing to be a coward. In this state of exhaustion, when my courage had almost gone, I determined to take my problem to God. My head in my hands, I bowed over the kitchen table and prayed aloud. The words I spoke to God that midnight are still vivid in my memory. "I am here taking a stand for what I believe is right. But now I am afraid. The people are looking to me for leadership, and if I stand before them without strength and courage, they too will falter. I am at the end of my powers. I have nothing left. I've come to the point where I can't face it alone."

At that moment I experienced the presence of the Divine as I had never before experienced him. It seemed as though I could hear the quiet assurance of an inner voice, saying, "Stand up for righteousness, stand up for truth. God will be at your side forever." Almost at once my fears began to pass from me. My uncertainty disappeared. I was ready to face anything. The outer situation remained the same, but God had given me inner calm.

Three nights later, our home was bombed. Strangely enough, I accepted the word of the bombing calmly. My experience with God had given me a new strength and trust. I knew now that God is able to give us the interior resources to face the storms and problems of life.[29]

Courage is what makes us able to go ahead and do what has to be done, despite our fear. Even Jesus experienced fear as the crucifixion loomed

---

[29] Martin Luther King, "Our God is Able," ed. James M. Washington, *A Testament of Hope: The Essential Writings of Martin Luther King, Jr.* (New York: Harper & Row, 1986), 508-9.

before him.　And yet, because of his obedience and courage, he drank from the cup that the Father had given him to drink.

Chapter 11

Look Back

This whole enterprise of discernment has two main benefits. One is that it gets us in sync with God's plans for us. The other is that it gives us a deeper sense of who God is, how he works, and how precious our relationship with him is. Looking back on what you asked God, what he revealed to you, how you followed his lead, how he provided, and what he was doing in the bigger picture is a rich and valuable experience.

Billy Graham, the great twentieth century evangelist, looked back through his autobiography, *Just As I Am.* From start to finish, he reminisces about the events of his life, the things God accomplished through him, and the way he sought God's guidance and God's strength. At the age of thirty, he was president of Northwestern Schools of Minneapolis, yet he describes himself as a simple country preacher.

The watershed event of his young life was the 1949 Los Angeles Evangelistic Campaign. The Los Angeles campaign was scheduled to be a three-week affair. Graham had what he thought were ambitious plans for the campaign and was able to persuade the local leadership to raise the budget from \$7,000 to \$25,000, erect a much larger tent than they had planned, and involve all the churches in Los Angeles. The media coverage was non-existent, prompting Graham to say in his autobiography, "As far as the media were concerned, the Los Angeles Campaign—by far our most ambitious evangelistic effort to date—was going to be a nonevent."[30]

As things turned out, the crusade started well, with four thousand people the first night, and grew in size and momentum. Graham and the other leaders continually sought God's guidance about extending the campaign. They asked God for signs and each time received them. Finally, after seventy-two meetings, the campaign closed at the end of the eighth week. The audience that night numbered eleven thousand. Hundreds of thousands had heard the Gospel, thousands had responded to accept Christ as Savior, of whom eighty-two percent had never been church members.[31] Billy reported in his book that his entire team was exhausted. The last few nights, he feared he would collapse at the pulpit. But, he said, "It seemed that

You will see a better view of the big picture than you had at the time.

____

[30] Billy Graham, *Just As I Am* (New York: Harper Collins, 1997), 143.
[31] Billy Graham, 157.

the weaker my body became, the more powerfully God used my simple words."[32]

Graham discovered over the next few weeks that this Los Angeles Campaign had national implications, which would define the future of his ministry and his life. In 1952, he resigned as president of Northwestern Schools. Again, reflecting on this phase of his life, he evaluates the hand of God in it. "Admittedly, I was never completely happy at Northwestern or totally convinced that I was in the will of God." He made it clear when he took the position that he had not received a prompting from God to do so, but wanted to be of help to the school during a difficult transition time. "As I look back now, however," he wrote in 1997, almost fifty years later, "I can see that many good things came of my time there, especially in the experience I gained in management and finances and in working with a board. The years there also gave me a greater understanding of young people. All of this would be valuable to me in future years."[33]

Every Christian who has served God according to God's plans has a treasure to look back upon. Such retrospection has several benefits.

First, it will bless you to have God open your eyes to what He did. You see a better view of the big picture than you had at the time. You may be

---

[32] Billy Graham, 156.
[33] Billy Graham, 121-2.

able to see how the events you were involved with played out in God's greater plan. And you will see how God used your willingness to be his servant. At the other end of the spectrum, you may see how things that seemed like small details at the time were strategic to God's work. You may see the miracles he did, for you will have a better handle on your own weaknesses and limitations after the fact than you would have been willing to acknowledge at the time. All of this will give you a sense of awe and excite you in your love of the Lord.

Second, as you look back, you will see the various ways God spoke to you. This may help your future discernment by giving you signs to look for. Does he give you visions or dreams? Does he put someone in your path to speak for him? Do you feel his peace when you are on the right track, as did John Wesley when he felt "strangely warmed?" Was it a sermon that opened your eyes and unstopped your ears? If so, you may want to put yourself in position frequently to hear deep biblical preaching—placing yourself in whatever environment for prayer and Bible study that most attuned you to God in the past.

> **Looking back will make you thankful that God chose you.**

Third, you will see patterns in the way God works in your life. Does he give you a lot of rope and then rescue you from time to time? Or does he give you a short rein and guide you at every step? How, as in Billy Graham's case, has God used your works that seemed outside his plan to equip and prepare you for future work within his plan?

And what about the Christian who has taken the wrong way? J.I. Packer offers us biblical encouragement.

> Our God is a God who not merely restores, but takes up our mistakes and follies into his plan for us and brings good out of them.... Guidance, like all God's acts of blessing under the covenant of grace, is a sovereign act. Not merely does God will to guide us in the sense of showing us his way, that we may tread it; he wills also to guide us in the more fundamental sense of assuring that, whatever happens, whatever mistakes we may make, we shall come safely home. Slippings and strayings there will be, no doubt, but the everlasting arms are beneath us, we shall be caught, rescued, restored. This is God's promise; this is how good he is.[34]

Fourth, as you look back, you will be able to assess your spiritual discipline. Maybe you will find that the reason God took so long to answer you was that you were hit-and-miss in your prayer and Scripture reading. Maybe you will see what kind of Scripture reading proved most effective in putting you on the proper wavelength to listen to God. Maybe you will see a pattern of sinful behavior that caused you to miscommunicate with

---

[34] J.I. Packer. *Knowing God* (Grove, IL: InterVarsity, 1993), 241-2.

God or doubt his willingness to use you. Maybe you will see where your fear paralyzed you and delayed your getting on track with God's plan.

Fifth, remembering the past will help you look to the future. Your life is a continuum. Everything that has happened in your past is a part of the same story as the events in your future. What you see in your past will affect how you think about the future. As the old saying goes, "God isn't done with you yet." You will see the price you paid for your obedience, and you will see that you made it through. Billy Graham said this about the last two grueling weeks of the Los Angeles Campaign: "Drained as I was, physically, mentally, and emotionally, I experienced God's unfailing grace in perpetual spiritual renewal."[35] Knowing God's faithfulness from your past experience can bolster your courage and obedience for your next deployment as his servant.

Sixth, looking back will make you thankful that God chose you. Seeing what great things he did, the way he communicated with you, and the way he empowered you and lifted you up when things became difficult is an occasion for saying, "Thank you, Lord, for placing such trust in your unworthy servant."

And finally, looking back is an occasion for celebrating the eternal quality of your life. As I said in Chapter 1, the life of the faithful disciple takes

---

[35] Billy Graham, 156

its quality from the living God. His Holy Spirit dwells within you. He takes joy in the salvation of souls. He takes joy in the love that his servants bestow on the least and the lost, and because you are his child, made in his image and heir to his kingdom, his joy is your joy. No longer is it the things of this world that are your greatest excitement; it is the things of God.

There is no greater gift, or joy, or satisfaction, than to work together with God as he redeems the world. The whole enterprise—from seeking to discern his plan for you; to hearing his voice, spoken to you in intimate communication; to obediently stepping out with courage; to relying on the guidance and empowerment of the Holy Spirit; to reflecting in awe—is a priceless treasure. May that treasure be yours. And may the glory be God's.

Appendix

A BIBLE STUDY FOR CORPORATE DISCERNMENT

**These meditations may be used
without permission or attribution.**

St. Stephen's Anglican Church
P.O. Box 609
Heathsville, Virginia 22473
804.580.4555

Hearing from God
September-October 2014

You and I are called by God to be his witnesses, to love our neighbors, and to take the Good News of Jesus Christ to all people near and far. How do we know what exactly to do? Do we get our plans from books? Do we do it the way another church we belonged to does it? Do we just do what feels good to us?

God has called us together as a church, he has given us special gifts, and he has a plan for us. It is therefore critical that we know what he wants us to do. That makes the question of hearing from God one of the key ones in our life as Christians. For us at St. Stephen's, this is a special time when we need to hear from God. We have been in a period of transition. What does God want us to learn from this? We have just begun work on a new worship and ministry facility that will be God's mission base for years to come. How does he want us to enter our new life in that space? Should we change our name, and if so, what should it be? We will soon have a second round of fundraising for the building. How much does God call us to give?

For the next few weeks, I will be preaching on "Hearing from God," and I ask you to engage in a daily practice of Bible Study, reading and reflecting on the Scriptures in this booklet. Let us follow God, trust him, and listen to him, for his glory and the good of all his Church.

Yours in Christ,

Jeffrey O. Cerar, Rector

Week 1
THE LORD SAYS, "FOLLOW ME."

This week's questions for personal reflection on each passage of scripture:

1. Whom did the Lord call?

2. In calling them to follow, what did He also call them to do?

3. What qualifications did they have?

4. What did the Lord offer as reassurance, if anything?

5. Do you have a personal story to share with your Bible study group?

Sunday
Genesis 12:1-8

God's perfect creation had been invaded by sin. A thorough house cleaning through the flood of Noah had left no change, other than God's covenant never again to destroy the world by flood. God moved to the next phase of his plan, which was to set apart a people of his own through whom his ultimate blessing would spread to the whole world. He picked a righteous man, who he knew was capable of heeding his call and following him—a man who would believe God and trust him. Abraham heard and followed. You and I are part of the multitudes of his descendants through whom God blesses the world. Faith. Trust.

Following God.   These are all in our fiber as disciples of Jesus Christ.

Monday
Exodus 3:1-12

Moses, a Hebrew raised in Pharaoh's household through the hand of the Lord, was hiding out in the far mountain wilderness of Sinai. Years before, he had murdered a man who was abusing a Hebrew slave. God now came to Moses and entreated Moses to follow him.   Moses was reluctant. He felt unworthy. He was afraid. He had many excuses. But God assured him and promised to be with him; and Moses followed— back to Egypt; back and forth speaking for God to Pharaoh; leading the people out of slavery and escaping through the miracle at the Red Sea; and shepherding them for forty years in the wilderness as God prepared them to enter the Promised Land. When we listen to God, he takes us where he wants and does amazing things with us.

Tuesday
Joshua 3:1-9

Joshua was Moses' trusted assistant. Of all those who had escaped from Egypt forty years earlier, only Joshua and Caleb were worthy to enter the promised land with all the Hebrew descendants. The Lord appeared to Joshua and told him that he was to be the new leader for this phase of God's plan. He was to lead them into Canaan. He was to lead the conquest as they settled in the land God was giving them. He, like Moses, didn't think he had what it took. God reassured Joshua and told him repeatedly, "Be strong and courageous." And God promised, "I will never leave you or forsake you." We too feel inadequate. We too must be strong and courageous to follow the Lord. And we too can trust that he will be with us always as Jesus promised in the Great Commission (Matthew 28:19-20).

Wednesday
Mark 1:16-20

Mark's account of Jesus' calling the first disciples is written in few words. It tells us just the facts. Jesus called Simon and Andrew, James and John, and said "Come follow me, and I will make you fishers of men." The call: follow me. The mission: fish for men. The promise: Jesus would transform them. Mark tells us Simon and Andrew left their nets and followed him "at once." He tells us James and John left their father Zebedee sitting right in the boat. The compulsion to follow Jesus must have been strong indeed. We are called "Christians," which means followers of Jesus Christ. Is that what we truly are? We have the same call, the same mission, and the same promise as those first disciples. Do we have the same compulsion?

Thursday
John 10:22-33

Jesus enjoyed portraying himself as a shepherd. Here in this passage, he is responding to those who challenged him to say whether he was the Messiah. He chided them for not knowing him. If you were my sheep, you would listen to me and follow me, he told them. We are Jesus' sheep, and he is our shepherd. Therefore, we follow him. And for us he has a special promise: "I give them eternal life, and they shall never perish; no one can snatch them out of my hand." Yes, indeed he was the Messiah – and not just the one to rescue God's people, but the King of kings and Lord of lords. "The Father and I are one," he said, and they wanted to stone him, for they considered that blasphemy. But he is our King and our Lord, and nothing can snatch us out of his hand. That is why we follow him so closely.

Friday
Luke 9:21-27

There is something in all of us that would like it to be easy to follow Jesus. In fact, many of us live as if it is easy, and thus we make little or no sacrifice, take little or no risk, and make few if any changes in the lifestyle we take from our culture. But Jesus said that if we want to be his disciple, we must deny ourselves, take up our cross daily, and follow him. When he said this, he was on his way to the cross. He had made the decision that the time had come to move in that direction. And so he is saying that we must go there with him, suffer with him, and be glorified with him. That word "follow" has a lot of content. It isn't like "following" the Orioles in their pennant race. It isn't like being a follower of our favorite pop star. It is a matter of being "all in" with the Son of God and Savior of the world. Are you a follower?

Saturday
Psalm 23

Long before Jesus, David understood how God is our shepherd, and we are the people of his pasture and the sheep of his hand. The 23rd Psalm is one of the most loved and memorized of all the psalms, because it projects the joy, the peace, the comfort and the confidence of being under the protective care of the King of kings and Lord of lords. As his sheep, we lack nothing. He leads us to where he provides nourishment for us. He prepares a feast for us. He gives us victory over the enemy. He walks with us through the darkest of times. He takes away our fears. His goodness and love flow through into every part of our lives. And he gives us our eternal dwelling. If faced with a choice to follow him or not, how could we not follow?

Week 2
THE LORD SAYS, "TRUST ME."

This week's questions for personal reflection on each passage of scripture:

1. Why does the Lord insist that we trust him?

2. Why is it hard to trust the Lord?

3. What does the Lord offer as encouragement in this passage?

4. Do you have a personal story on trusting the Lord and what the result was?

Sunday
Judges 7:1-8

Gideon is a fearful nobody from a no-account family. Yet God appoints him to lead the conquest of Canaan and give him glorious victories over the Midianites. In Chapter 6, God comes to Gideon while he is hiding out, and commissions him. Gideon protests his inability, and when God persists, Gideon asks for signs. Finally, Gideon is on board, and in Chapter 7, God dramatically directs him to pare down the army, so that there will be only three hundred soldiers to face the many thousand Midianites. God wants the message of victory to come through loud and clear: It is God's strength and God's power that saves. Imagine how hard it was for Gideon to trust God with his small detachment of three hundred against the hordes of "Midian with tents like swarms of locusts," and men and camels too many to count (Judges 6:5-6).

Monday
Genesis 6:9-22

Noah was another unsuspecting man for whom God had a plan. Everyone knows the story. God said he would destroy the world, and he told Noah to build an ark. He gave Noah detailed instructions. And Noah did as God had told him. As the story gets retold, great emphasis is placed on the animals, and Noah is always portrayed as a laughingstock among his neighbors. The Bible doesn't say that, but it is safe to assume that their abject corruption and disregard for God caused them to find Noah's righteous behavior to be a joke, maybe a throwback to a "less enlightened time." As God's people, we think of the pressure on Noah to continue with the project, make the necessary sacrifices, and endure the ridicule, based solely on believing what God had told him. That is called faith. That is trust.

Tuesday
Genesis 15:1-7

Last week we read the call of Abraham. Did you ever wonder why God didn't just transport Abraham to Canaan himself, and tell him his plans after Abraham had moved? God wanted Abraham to believe him and to trust him. Three chapters later, Abraham went to the Promised Land, but he still didn't have the heir God had promised him. When he reminded God about that, God simply told him that he would have a son coming from his own body.   The Bible tells us that "Abraham believed the Lord, and he credited it to him as righteousness" (Genesis. 15:6).   *Righteous* means "in right standing with God." Believing him is what God seeks from us.   Abraham had moments when he needed a sign from God, and moments when he took things into his own hands.   But he believed God.

Wednesday
Exodus 16:9-26

How could over a million wandering Hebrews survive in the Sinai desert for forty years without God's direct intervention?   They had no choice but to trust him for their food and water.   They were at God's mercy out there, and if he failed them, they were dead.   And yet, even as they survived from day to day, they grumbled.   This story of the manna emphasizes that God was responding to their grumbling.   And it also shows us that God wasn't finished demanding their trust.   Manna, though a miraculous substance, spoiled after one day.   So each day, they could gather only enough for one day's food, even though it lay in abundance on the desert floor.   God would not allow them to stockpile his blessing in fear that one day he would no longer bless them.

Thursday
Romans 8:28-39

These verses are the last ascent to the summit of this majestic chapter of hope and glory. Are you in a position to believe all that it says? Do you trust God enough to believe that in all things he works for the good of those who love him and are called according to his purpose? Do you take comfort in knowing that since God gave the greatest gift of his Son, he will give you all things? Are you undamaged by the accusations and condemnations of the world because God has found you worthy? Do you know in your heart that nothing in all creation can separate you from the love of God in Christ? If you can answer all these questions in the affirmative, your spirit must be soaring, and your life must be filled with thankfulness and joy. And you must truly trust God. Wait till you see what he will do with those who trust Him.

Friday
Joshua 1:1-9

When we put our trust in God, he will do things with us that stretch us. That is why in so many places in the Bible, we hear God or an angel tell someone to be strong and courageous, or to "fear not," or to be reminded that nothing is impossible with God. In this passage, God tells Joshua three times to be strong and courageous. What is he saying? He's not saying, "If you are strong enough, you can do this." He's not saying, "If you have enough guts, you can do this." He is really saying, "Trust me, and we'll do this together. It's going to be hard for you to keep on trusting me because you will be tempted to see it through worldly eyes. So hang in there and let me do what I do. Be strong enough not to give up. Be courageous enough to be my transportation to the fray."

Saturday
Malachi 3:6-12

In this passage, God says again, "Trust me." Actually, his words are, "Test me in this." Nowhere else in the Bible does God tell us to test him. In fact, Jesus told Satan that it is written (in Deuteronomy 6:16), "You shall not put the Lord your God to the test." But in Malachi, God was rebuking his people. They were cheating on the tithe, and he was not happy. He took it as a sign that they did not trust him to provide for them. And so he says these indelible words: "Bring the whole tithe...and see if I do not throw open the floodgates of heaven and pour out so much blessing that you will not have room enough for it." Just as in all the readings this week, we see God saying, "I have things I want to do. I choose to have someone to work with. Trust me, and you will see miracles."

Week 3

THE LORD SAYS, "LET GO."

This week's questions for personal reflection on each passage of scripture:

1. What human tendency do you see in this passage?

2. How does it get in the way of God's people doing what he calls them to do?

3. Is this a demand or an invitation?

4. What does the Lord promise his people in this incident?

5. How are letting go and trusting in God related?

6. Do you have a personal story to share?

Sunday
Numbers 11:1-6

Once again, we are in the desert with the Hebrew people, eating manna. And now we hear their response. They are complaining about the manna, and they are looking back to Egypt where they seem to say they had it so good! Egypt! The place where they were slaves, suffering under the lash of the taskmaster as they built Pharaoh's pyramids. It was God's deliverance from this slavery that they celebrated at Passover, and it had become their self-defining story. But they made faces at their dinner and longed for the past. Have you been there, done that? If so, you probably did not recognize it at the time. We recognize our ingratitude and churlish behavior in retrospect. But in the moment, it is possible to look inward and ask ourselves, what am I hanging onto that I need to let go of?

Monday
Matthew 6:19-34

This is from the Sermon on the Mount, where Jesus is introducing his listeners to a new way of life—one that is steeped in God's values, God's provision and God's promises. It is a heaven-oriented way of life. In this passage, Jesus contrasts the temporary nature of things on earth with the things of eternal worth. He tells us we have to choose whom we are going to serve. He exhorts us not to be anxious for our needs, for God will provide. And he tells us to seek the Kingdom of God rather than dwell on the things of this earth. Jesus wants to be our focus, our priority and our desire. This will require that other things lose their importance to us and fade off into insignificance by comparison. Paul understood it: "I consider everything as loss compared to the surpassing greatness of knowing Christ Jesus my Lord" (Philippians 3:8).

Tuesday
Matthew 8:18-27

Are these two stories, or one? In the first part, Jesus makes the point that following him is not something that comes without sacrifice. A teacher of the Law said he would follow Jesus anywhere. Instead of praising the man's intentions, Jesus told him in essence to be careful what he asks for; the Son of Man has nowhere to lay his head. Another said he wanted to follow, but had family needs to attend to first. Jesus told him to let that go and follow him. Then came the incident of the furious storm that threatened to sink the boat in which Jesus and the disciples were traveling. Jesus slept calmly, while the disciples feared for their lives. In terror, they woke him up and begged him to save them from drowning. His response? "Oh you of little faith, why are you so afraid?" What do you see that ties these incidents together as one message from Jesus?

Wednesday
Matthew 19:16-30

There is a lot in this story of the rich young man. He was seeking eternal life and asked Jesus how to gain it. Jesus spoke of the Jewish way: Keeping God's law will give you fullness of life. But the man had tried that. So Jesus told him the only sure way, "Follow me." And in order to make that possible for this rich young man, he was going to have to give up all his riches. That was too much to ask, for he went away sad. Then Jesus turned to his disciples and pointed out what they had just seen: It is very hard for a rich person to let all that go to follow Jesus. This astounded them, for the rich were esteemed as those whom God had blessed. And Jesus answered that only God can save, and for him all things are possible. And then he acknowledged their sacrifice and assured them of their inheritance.

Thursday
Luke 9:1-6

It was time for the disciples to try what they had seen Jesus do. He sent them out to the towns and villages. Their mission was to preach the Kingdom of God, to heal the sick, and to cast out evil. How did he equip them for the mission? He gave them authority, and he sent the power of the Holy Spirit with them. That's it. He told them, "Take nothing for the journey..." He didn't want them taking all kinds of worldly provisions to weigh them down, give a false sense of security, and distract them. He also told them to rely on the hospitality of the people to whom they went to minister. They would be at the mercy of their hosts. Some would refuse to welcome them, and that was not to dissuade them.   Jesus wanted it to be clear where their strength and provision was coming from.

Friday
Luke 21:10-19

This is Luke's version of the apocalyptic sermon Jesus gave the disciples shortly before the Last Supper, betrayal and crucifixion occurred. He was preparing them for the final days when things would be in great upheaval, when he would come in glory to judge the living and the dead. It would be a frightening time to which no one would look forward, even the faithful followers of Jesus. It would be the death throes of evil and it wouldn't be pretty. He described some of the things the disciples would have to face, including being hauled before tribunals as if they were criminals. They would be required to speak for their faith in Jesus. And from whence would their help come? When you are tempted to worry about it, let it go. He said. "I will give you words and wisdom that none of your adversaries will be able to resist or contradict."

Saturday
Philippians 4:10-13

The flip side of letting go is being content. Paul gives us the definitive statement on contentment in this passage from Philippians: "I have learned the secret of being content in all circumstances." As he recites here, he has seen it all. He has been loved and hated. He has been in need and well fed. He has lived in plenty and in want. In fact, elsewhere, he describes the many things he suffered as an apostle for Jesus Christ (2 Corinthians 11:16-29): beatings, imprisonments, hunger, thirst and shipwrecks. Interestingly, in our Philippians passage, Paul doesn't reveal the "secret" of contentment. But he ends this part of his letter by saying, "I can do all things through him who strengthens me." And in another place, he quotes Jesus as saying, "My grace is sufficient for you" (2 Corinthians 12:9). This is "letting go and letting God," as the saying goes.

Week 4
THE LORD SAYS, "LISTEN TO ME."

This week's questions for personal reflection on each passage of scripture:

1. What does effective listening require?

2. What additionally do we need in order to listen effectively to the Lord?

3. Why is it so important to listen for God's voice?

4. What are some different ways the Lord speaks to us?

5. Do you have a personal story to share?

Sunday
Matthew 17:1-8

This "mountaintop experience" was a key moment in Jesus' life with the disciples and in his earthly mission. It was just six days after Peter's confession of Jesus as the Messiah and the Son of the Living God, and Jesus' rebuke of Peter for challenging Jesus' revelation that he must go to the cross. Here on the mountain, for a brief moment, Peter, James and John, who had gone up there with him, were able to see his glory. He also appeared with Moses and Elijah, putting Jesus in an eternal context for them to consider. And then the Father spoke a crucial message: "This is my beloved Son, in whom I am well pleased; listen to Him." Don't doubt who Jesus is. And listen to what he has to say, for he has the words of eternal life.

Monday
Jeremiah 29:10-14

God knew when the time of the exile of the Hebrew people would end. They didn't know. In fact, they did not know if it would ever end. How was God going to communicate his plans to his people? He is speaking through the prophet, Jeremiah, giving them the reassuring news that he had good plans for them. And now he calls upon them to seek him out. "If you will call upon me and come and pray to me," God said, "I will listen to you." And he said that if they seek him with all their heart, they will find him. He will listen to them, and he will speak. If they will listen to him, they will know what God is doing. It is the same with God's people today.

He wants to communicate with us. He wants us to seek him out and listen to Him.

Tuesday
John 10:1-11

In this passage, Jesus speaks of himself as the Good Shepherd. A good shepherd is devoted to his sheep and lays down his life for his sheep. And more than that, he has a personal relationship with the sheep in his charge. He knows each one by name. The shepherd talks to them, and they come to recognize his voice. It becomes so familiar to them that they can tell when a stranger is trying to impose himself on them. And when their own shepherd speaks to them, they listen to him. Jesus is after that kind of closeness with us. He wants us to know his voice so well that we can tell an impostor when we hear one. And he wants us to turn our heads to him when he speaks. He wants us to listen to him, for he has much to say to us.

Wednesday
I Samuel 3:1-21

Before Samuel was conceived, his mother had made a promise to God that she would set her son apart to serve him. Here, Samuel is a boy, apprenticed to Eli the priest. He has been helping out and learning the ropes of being God's representative with the people. On this night, God is seeking to speak to Samuel for the first time. The boy doesn't recognize it as God's voice. He thinks it must be Eli. The old priest finally figures out what is going on, and he advises Samuel what he must do to be obedient. He is to wait until God calls again, as Eli knows He will. And when God calls, Samuel is to say, "Speak, Lord, for your servant is listening." Obedience and listening are essentials for becoming a faithful servant of the Lord, as Samuel was. As the scripture tells us, "The Lord was with him as he grew."

Thursday
Deuteronomy 4:25-31

One more time, we are in the Torah, and Moses is speaking to the Hebrew people as they are poised at last to enter the Promised Land. It's been a long wait, a long time of learning and discipline. The message is a warning of what will happen if the people forget God after they have received his promise and lived in Canaan for a couple of generations. They will perish, they will be scattered, and they will worship false gods. But, if instead they seek God with all their heart, they will find Him. That is a promise. Moses tells them that undoubtedly they will stray from God. But he also says they will turn back to God in their distress, and obey him once again. God is merciful, and he is true to his everlasting covenant with them. Listen to his warning. Listen to his reassurance. Listen to his commands.

Friday
Revelation 3:14-22

In Jesus' revelation to the Apostle John, he shows John many vivid, frightening and wonderful things. He also gives John a message for the seven churches under his charge as Bishop of Asia Minor. These messages are eternal messages for the Church. The one for the congregation in Laodicea is meant to awaken them from their false image of themselves. He rebukes them for their tepid faith. In fact, He says, "I wish you were hot or cold.... Because you are lukewarm, I spit you out of my mouth!" You can't help but hope they were listening. Jesus made an unforgettable plea, saying he is standing at the door knocking, and whoever hears his voice and lets him in will be blessed by his joining them at the table. And he ends with this repeated message: "Whoever has an ear, let him hear."

Saturday
I Kings 19:9-18

The great prophet Elijah was just a man. He had become fearful for his life because the dreaded Queen Jezebel had said she was going to kill him. It was just on the heels of Elijah's great triumph on the mountaintop, where he defeated the prophets of Baal and exposed their god as a false god. He ran away to hide and ended up in a cave on a faraway mountain. God found him there, of course, and demanded an audience with him. God was not subtle in telling Elijah what to do to put himself in a position to hear what God wanted to say to him. And yet, when he came, God spoke in a "gentle whisper," or a "still, small voice." Sometimes, we have to quiet ourselves dramatically to hear God speaking to us. But whatever it takes, it is essential that we do it. For the God of all creation wants to communicate with us.

BIBLIOGRAPHY

Augustine of Hippo. *The Confessions of St. Augustine.* Translated by J. Ryan. New York, NY: Image Books, Doubleday, 1960.

Aylward, G. with C. Hunter, *The Little Woman.* Chicago, IL: Moody, 1970.

Blackaby, H., R. Blackaby and C. King, *Experiencing God* (Workbook). Nashville, TN: Lifeway Press, 2007.

Calvin, John. *Institutes of the Christian Religion.* Translated from Latin to English in 1845 by Henry Beveridge. www.biblestudytools.com/history/calvin-institutes-Christianity.

Colson, Charles. *Born Again.* Grand Rapids, MI: Chosen Books, Baker Publishing Co., 2008.

Cymbala, Jim. *Fresh Wind, Fresh Fire.* Grand Rapids, MI: Zondervan, 1997.

Cymbala, Jim. *Fresh Power.* Grand Rapids, MI: Zondervan, 2003.

Edwards, Jonathan. *An American Revival - An Account of a Surprising Move of God.* Goodyear, AZ: Diggory Press, 2007.

Foster, Richard. *Celebration of Discipline - The Path to Spiritual Growth.* San Francisco, CA: Harper, Revised Edition, 1988.

Foster, Richard. *Prayer - Finding the Heart's True Home.* San Francisco, CA: Harper, 1992.

Galli, Mark and Ted Olsen. *131 Christians Everyone Should Know.* Nashville, TN: Broadman & Holman, 2000.

Graham, Billy. *Just As I Am.* New York, NY: Harper Collins, 1997.

Grudem, Wayne. *Systematic Theology.* Grand Rapids, MI: Zondervan, 1994.

Guiness, Os. *The Call.* Nashville, TN: Thomas Nelson, 2003.

King, Martin Luther, Jr. *A Testament of Hope - The essential Writings of Martin Luther King, Jr.* Edited by James M. Washington. New York, NY: Harper & Row, 1986.

Marshall, Catherine. *A Man Called Peter.* New York, NY: McGraw Hill, 1951.

Nevisa, Mina. *Miracle of Miracles.* Fairfax, VA: Touch of Christ Ministries, 2004.

Packer, J.I. *God's Plans for You.* Wheaton, IL: Crossway, 2001.

Packer, J.I. *Knowing God.* Downers Grove, IL: InterVarsity, 1993.

Packer, J.I. and C. Nystrom. *Praying - Finding Our Way Through Duty to Delight.* Downers Grove, IL: InterVarsity Press, 2006.

Stott, John. *The Contemporary Christian.* Downers Grove, IL: InterVarsity Press, 1992.

Stott, John/ *The Radical Disciple - Some Neglected Aspects of Our Calling.* Downers Grove, IL: InterVarsity Press, 2010.

Tozer, A.W. *Culture - Living as Citizens of Heaven on Earth.* Chicago, IL: Moody Publishers, 2016.

Tozer, A.W. *God's Pursuit of Man*. Chicago, IL: Mood Publishers, 2015.

Tozer, A.W. *Mystery of the Holy Spirit.* Alachua, FL: Bridge-Logos, 2007.

Tozer, A.W. *The Pursuit of God.* Abbotsford, WI: Aneko Press, 2015.

Made in the USA
Middletown, DE
08 September 2017